The Rise & Fall of Nottingham's Railway Network

Volume 2

Beyond the City Limits

Hayden J Reed

To my wife, for putting up with the trains where my parents left off.

Contents

Introduction

This is the second of two volumes that chart the history of Nottingham's railways. It looks at the lines leading to the City, from their early beginnings through to the decimation of the network in the wake of the Beeching Report and beyond. Nottingham once sat at the hub of a complex rail system and at its peak, four national companies operated out of the City. Cross-country routes radiated out in all directions of the compass, and freight concentration yards sprang up to handle the vast quantities of materials being shipped by rail. Economic trends, shifting modes of transport and politics have progressively eroded this network and a century on, most of it has disappeared.

A number of books have been published about Nottingham's railways over the years, but the more peripheral lines have in some respects been neglected. This work has set out to cover both the City and the surrounding area, combining historical and technical aspects with anecdotes, an extensive photographic record and explanatory plans.

The Author grew up in Nottingham in the Sixties and Seventies, when derelict rail routes still criss-crossed the City and its suburbs. Fascinated by disused structures and abandoned track beds, he began photographing them from his early teens. The interest has followed him through two decades of working as a Civil Engineer for Nottingham's Highway Authority.

In the course of his career the Author has gained access to many places inaccessible to the general public. This has enabled him to record images of numerous Victorian railway structures that have since been demolished or buried and forgotten. The resulting archive, supported with previously unpublished photographs of the network in its heyday, historic material, plans and diagrams has been brought together to create a unique record of the rise, decline and ultimate fall of Nottingham's railway network.

The first volume took a look at railway lines that fell within the main City area (within the central box on the map opposite).

Volume Two covers areas from the outer limits of Nottingham to either the County boundary, or to a radius of about ten miles from the City. The primary reason for this stems from the Author's initial photographic record being limited to how far he could reasonably cycle from where he lived on the east side of the City.

The photographs in this work are primarily the Author's own work, but where other Photographers material has been kindly loaned, these have been credited as appropriate. All network maps and diagrams are copyrighted to the Author.

H J Reed, March 2007.

Right : The GNR/LNWR Joint line from Saxondale was just one of many route miles to be abandoned in the wake of the Beeching cuts. The greater part of these disused routes have now been built over or returned to farmland, leaving remarkably little left of what was once a very extensive network.

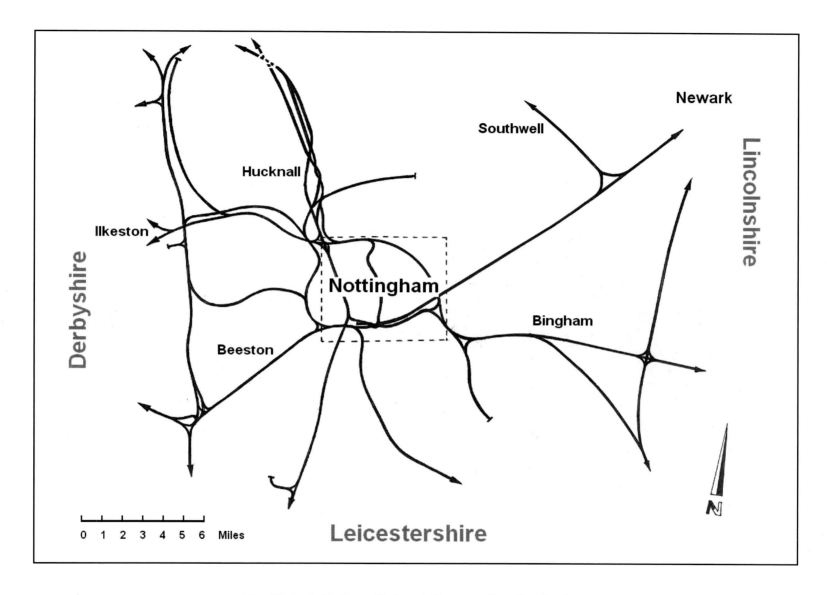

The Historic Railway Network Surrounding Nottingham

Nottingham once sat at the hub of a substantial railway network, as the plan above shows. Much of it was built during the latter part of the Nineteenth century when "Railwaymania" gripped the country, and rival companies were scrambling to reach the same markets. In the Twenty first Century, very little of this labyrinth now exists. Volume One explored the rise and fall of the railways within "metropolitan" Nottingham (shown in the central box). Volume Two takes a look at the wider picture, and those lines that ran beyond the immediate City limits.

1. The Midland Counties Railway
Lenton South Junction to Trent Junction

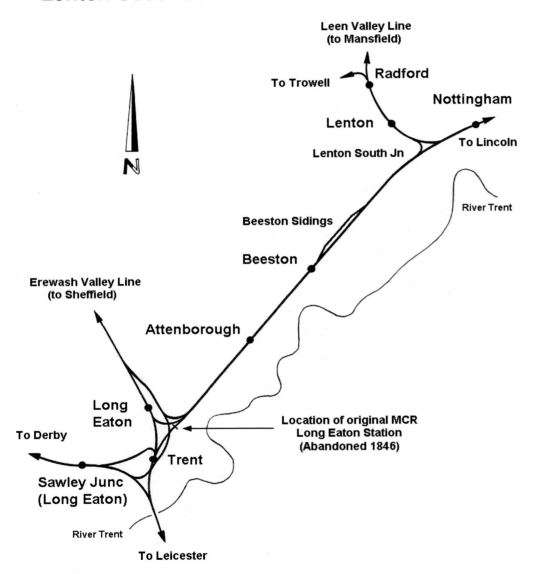

The diagram above shows the route of the MCR between Lenton Junction and Trent, as it existed in about 1900. The junction arrangement at Trent was one of the most complex in the area, with individual lines converging from five separate directions.

The Railway Age truly dawned for Nottingham on the 30th May 1839, when the Midland Counties Railway's line to Derby opened. Before this the only railways in the Nottingham area were plateways connecting collieries and quarries with the canal network and the River Trent. Nothing existed that was recognisable as a modern railway, and no public services existed for the conveyance of passengers overland, other than by horse drawn coach.

The MCR had set about construction of this venture in May 1838, having obtained Parliamentary powers in 1836. Two railway lines were built consecutively, the first 16 mile line from Derby to Nottingham, and the second from a junction near Long Eaton, south to Leicester.

When first opened the line was twin throughout, following the flat ground of the Trent flood plain. This reduced the need for structures and earthworks, and hence the overall cost. When first opened, there were no junctions, since there was no network to speak of. Long Eaton Junction came into existence shortly after, with completion of the second phase of the project to Leicester. This junction would expand and come to be known as Trent Junction in the years to come, and an interchange station would eventually be built there.

Johnson passenger tank No 1257 is seen resting between duties near Trent in about 1920.

H E L Tatham

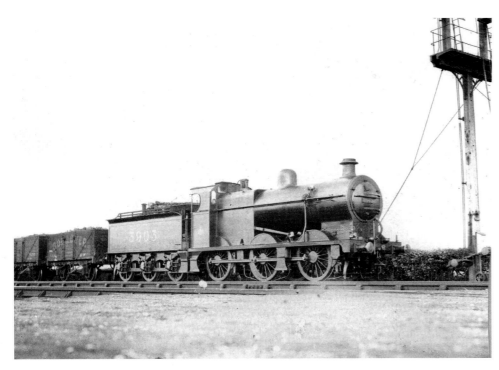

Class 4F No 3903 is seen above, with a loose coupled freight at a signal check near Trent. The loaded wagon from Bolsover Colliery suggests that this is a southbound working originating from the Erewash Valley line.

H E L Tatham

A Class 2P rounds the curve at Sheet Stores Junction, to the West of Trent with a local train in 1956. The rural character of the location is evident in this view.

C A Hill

Lenton South Junction was built in 1848, four years after the MCR had amalgamated with the North Midland and Birmingham & Derby Junction Railways to form the Midland Railway. Lenton South Junction formed the south west corner of a triangular junction, with the new Leen Valley line heading north towards Mansfield.

There were eventually four stations between Trent and Lenton Junctions, these being located at Trent, Long Eaton, Beeston and Attenborough. The first of these was built purely as an interchange, and served no community, sitting isolated in the open countryside, surrounded by lines and junctions. Constructed relatively late in the life of the line, it was opened in 1862, and built as part of a major junction remodelling exercise. The station consisted of a wide single island platform, with a substantial block of brick built buildings, flanked by ornate wrought iron canopies to each side.

The MCR only built one station on this stretch of line at Long Eaton. This station had a relatively short life, and was replaced by the Midland Railway in 1847 with a more conveniently located one on the newly built Erewash Valley line.

The remaining two stations at Attenborough and Beeston were opened in 1862 and 1847 respectively. Attenborough was little more than a halt, with facing platforms, level crossing to one end, and fairly basic shelters. No goods yard was provided, although a siding connected with nearby gravel works. Beeston Station was more substantial, reflecting the larger community that it served. The principal buildings were located on the north platform. These elegantly proportioned structures were built in yellow brick and provided with finely detailed wrought and cast iron canopies. Timber shelters occupied much of the length of the facing platforms, protecting passengers from the elements. A sizeable goods yard and single road goods shed was built to the east of the station, beyond a level crossing.

Development of the line was rapid, and industry sprang up alongside the line, requiring sidings and connections. At Beeston, extensive sidings were built to the north east of the station, to service traffic generated by the extensive industrial base that grew up in the area. At Chilwell the Government built an extensive Ordnance depot, and a connection was made to the extensive private rail network that formed part of this facility. Eventually significant traffic would be moved by rail from this facility, particularly during the two World Wars.

An unidentified Johnson tank heads a Nottingham-Derby service bunker first , near Attenborough in around 1920.

H E L Tatham

A Kirtley 890 Class is in charge of a respectable load as it passes near Attenborough, some time shortly after the Great War.

H E L Tatham

The line was equipped with block signalling in the 1880s, and standard Midland pattern signal boxes appeared together with the characteristic lower quadrant semaphore signals on yellow posts. Traffic was considerable, and Lenton South Junction Signal Box became so busy that it became the only box in the Nottingham area to be re-equipped with Rotary Interlocking block instruments, as opposed to traditional latch operated equipment. The Rotary Interlocking block instrument was patented by the Midland Railway at the start of the Twentieth Century, and internal mechanical latches made operator error virtually impossible. It was suited it to boxes handling large volumes of traffic, but was more expensive to manufacture than conventional instruments, which meant that the Company was selective in where it introduced them.

Lenton South Junction marked not only the western divergence of the Leen Valley route from the Nottingham – Derby line, but also the point that Clifton Colliery traffic took access. The later construction of Wilford Power Station next to the colliery resulted in much of the production being used rather than shipped out onto the main line. Nonetheless Lenton South was to remain one of the busier parts of the local network.

Freight traffic on the line continued to grow until after the First World War. The depression years saw traffic start to slump. The Second World War years, and the creation of a major industrial estate centred around the Boots Company's works boosted traffic and Beeston Sidings developed into a major staging point. The move away from traditional small wagon haulage resulted in the closure of Beeston's station goods yard to general merchandise traffic. Beeston Sidings remained in use, but declining manufacturing and shift towards road transport for goods distribution resulted in a downturn in freight traffic. This was not quite the end of freight on the railway however. In order to modernise and compete with road transport, British Rail constructed a Freightliner terminal at the western end of Beeston Sidings. This continues in use today, but much of the original sidings at Beeston lie derelict and part of the site has even been classified as a nature reserve. Wilford Power Station and Clifton Colliery are also gone, and today freight forms a smaller proportion of traffic on the line than passenger diagrams.

Passenger revenues also fell into decline through the latter part of the Twentieth Century, in common trends across the national rail network. In the years after the Second World War the spread of motor bus services, and then the explosion in private car ownership bit deeply into passenger figures.

The signal is at clear as a 2P accelerates away from Attenborough Station with a Nottingham train. The station footbridge is just visible in the background of this photograph which dates from about 1920.

H E L Tatham

Viewed from the doorway of Lenton South Junction Signal Box, a train from Derby in the charge of a Johnson tank takes the Nottingham Line. By an unknown photographer, this view dates from around the time of the First World War.

Authors Collection

In response to declining patronage local services were progressively pruned, and the Beeching Report of 1962 spelt the end of Long Eaton and Trent Stations altogether. Commuter traffic was sufficient to allow Beeston and Attenborough Stations to remain open, although Attenborough was to become an unstaffed halt.

Trent Junction Station closed in 1968, the need for connections having been dispensed with. The station was demolished immediately after, and no traces of it remain today. With the removal of the station, the track plan was rationalised, and several elements removed, including the North Curve which had been part of the original MCR alignment. Today the site of this is occupied by a road and housing estate. The name of Trent lives on however. A new regional power signal box of that name was opened there in 1969. This box controls signalling across much of the Nottingham and Derby area, and its commissioning allowed removal of most of the traditional block post signal boxes.

Trent Power Box itself is now due for replacement, and at the time of writing, plans are being drawn up for wholesale resignalling works. The replacement of Trent will see the end of several mechanical boxes in the area, including Sneinton Junction, Netherfield Junction and Rectory Junction. It will however provide extra train capacity and equip the remaining network for the demands of operation in the Twenty First Century.

Lenton South Junction box was equipped with the Midland Railway's unique Rotary Interlocking block instruments. An example is seen here in the middle. The handle in the centre of the brass disc is rotated clockwise to send indications to the next block post,

Lenton South Junction is seen here in 1988. The line on the right fed Clifton Colliery, and was lifted a few years after the photograph was taken. The ROD gun factory in the distance and the steel footbridge on the right have also gone.

By 2006 Beeston goods yard had been cleared of tracks, and stood awaiting redevelopment. It had closed to general merchandise traffic in the Sixties, but continued as private sidings right up to the start of the twenty first century.

The late Eighties were a time of transition. By 1988 "Peaks" were becoming a rarity and it was unusual to see a single Class 20 in traffic. Both are seen here to the south of Lenton Junction, with 45140 running light engine past an unidentified Class 20 on an Engineers working.

Beeston Station has fared remarkably well over the years, and still has a ticket office. Built in 1847 by the Midland Railway, it continues to see substantial commuter use.

A Nottingham bound Class 170 departs Beeston on 4th February 2006. The remarkable state of preservation of the station is evident here, with only the motive power giving away the date.

Attenborough Station was modernised in the late Sixties, and the original buildings removed. The original footbridge remains, but today the station lacks even platform shelters.

The bridge to the east of the station was constructed in the Sixties to replace the level crossing and original wrought iron footbridge. The old crossing is seen here some time before the Great War. The Photographers details are not known, but the view includes a Johnson tank that has just been given a clear signal. The starter signal has a high level bracketed co-acting arm.

Author's Collection

One reminder of the past at Attenborough is the lower portion of the signal box, which was converted to an equipment room when the box was abolished in 1982.

2.0 Railways around the Erewash

The River Erewash runs along the boundary between Nottinghamshire and Derbyshire, rising to the south west of Kirkby in Ashfield and flowing south to join the River Trent at Attenborough. The broad flat bottomed valley of the River Erewash is fertile agricultural land. Numerous settlements were recorded here in the Domesday Book of 1089, and doubtless occupation dates back to considerably earlier.

Beneath the fields and meadows lay another resource that was to transform the fortunes of the region. Coal had been known about in the northern reaches of the Erewash Valley for a long time, but in common with the Leen Valley it wasn't until the 18th Century that it was commercially exploited. The area wholeheartedly embraced the industrial revolution, and by the start of the 19th Century, mining, iron founding, textiles and the ceramics industry had all become firmly established. Previously rural communities like Eastwood, Ilkeston and Kimberley were transformed into mini industrial boom towns, to be later described in the writings of D.H. Lawrence.

These industries had been serviced in the 18th Century by canals, but as the 19th Century progressed they were gradually supplanted by the railways. Two companies, the Midland and The Great Northern battled for patronage. A web of lines and private industrial branches sprang up, and by the First World War there were few points in The Erewash Valley from which a railway line could not be seen or heard.

Inevitably coal that could be easily reached by conventional mining gradually worked out. Pit closures began as early as the late Nineteenth Century and the process accelerated as the Twentieth Century progressed. Ironworks needing local coal for their furnaces came under pressure from this and growing foreign competition. Many closed, whilst others amalgamated under the ownership of Stanton & Staveley. By the end of the Twentieth Century deep mining had all but finished in the Erewash Valley, a victim of economics and politics, to be replaced by retail outlets, warehousing and theme parks. With the exception of the Midland line, the railways had gone too. Stanton & Staveley continue to represent heavy industry in the area, as do the steel fabricators Butterley, but locally generated railway freight today is a fraction of what it once was.

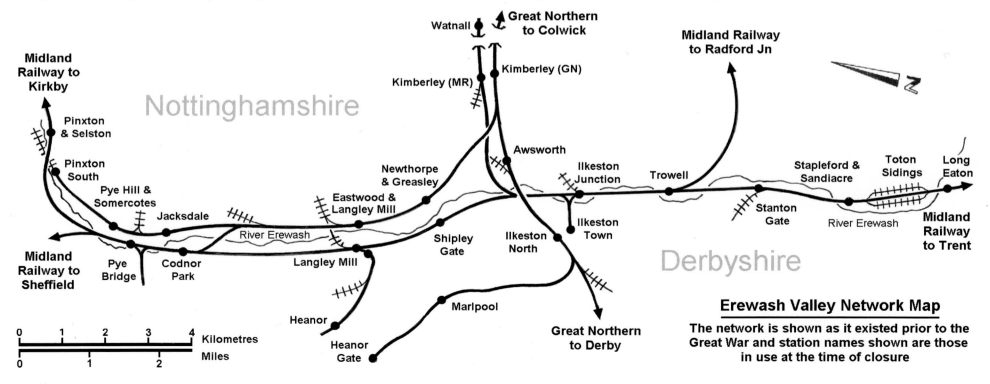

Erewash Valley Network Map

The network is shown as it existed prior to the Great War and station names shown are those in use at the time of closure

2.1 The Midland Railway's Main Line

The Midland Railway's principal route from Sheffield to St Pancras bypassed Nottingham, passing to the west of the City. The Erewash Valley element of the route dated from 1847 and was built north from the original Midland Counties line at Trent Junction. Branches were added to serve the local population centres at Ilkeston and Heanor. Further freight lines accessed local collieries and foundries, and the products of Stanton Ironworks contributed substantially to traffic. The relatively gentle topography meant that few large structures were required, although the addition of freight lines required multiple span overbridges.

Johnson six coupled goods No 2984 is seen on a freight working on the Erewash Valley line in around 1920. The photograph is believed to be south of Trowell Junction.

H E L Tatham

To the southern end of the Erewash Valley, at Toton near Stapleford, the Midland built marshalling yards to handle and distribute the diverse goods generated across the area. Locomotive sheds were also needed to provide the motive power to move the freight. The Midland Railway's small engine policy meant that additional engines were required to double head the heavier trains. Consequently the depot was built with very substantial facilities to service the large fleet of freight engines it needed. Toton was well placed on the Midland's network, situated midway between Nottingham and Derby, with direct connections to London and the north. The yards and depot were expanded and modernised several times under Midland, LMS and latterly British Rail ownership.

After BR's restructuring in the late Fifties, the London Midland Region gained control of the rival regional distribution centre at Colwick. As freight traffic slipped into decline LMR management progressively redirected business into Toton, ensuring survival of the facility, at Colwick's expense.

Ex LMS Garratt No 47998 is seen at Toton Depot resting between duties in 1956. The class were closely associated with Toton, from their introduction in 1927, through to withdrawal of the last survivor in 1960.

C A Hill

A more recent view of Toton Depot taken in 1978 reveals first and second generation diesel power on shed. The original steam facilities were rebuilt completely in the 1960s.

C A Hill

The closure of Colwick in 1970 left Toton as the principal facility in the area, but changing trends in freight movement have continued to see traffic decline. At present the yard is still used, but is now a shadow of its former self, with many of the sidings overgrown and out of use. Toton Depot is the last traditional shed in the immediate Nottingham area to remain open. The loss of the Nottinghamshire coalfield in the Eighties led to a decline in the need for locomotive haulage in the area and Toton's allocation suffered accordingly. Privatisation and changing ways of haulage procurement have also had their effect and the future of the Depot is far from certain.

A classic view of a Matthew Kirtley designed goods locomotive. No 2438 is seen with a mixed freight on the southern portion of the Erewash Valley line in about 1920.

H E L Tatham

An unidentified Class 47 heads south with a rake of 100 tonne tankers past the site of Trowell Station. By the time this picture was taken in 1983, no trace remained of the one time busy junction station.

National rail strategy and long distance traffic may have assured the trunk Midland line's future, but declining local revenues saw an end to all of the Midland branch lines in the Erewash Valley area during the Sixties. This era also saw total loss of every station in the area, including those on the main line.

In the two decades that followed Beeching, it became apparent that the network had been over-pruned. Public demand for rail services and pressure from Local Authorities led in 1984 to the construction of a new station at Langley Mill, to replace the one closed in the Sixties. The Erewash Valley was connected once more with Nottingham, Derby and London.

Stanton Ironworks were an important employer in the Erewash Valley and owned a string of sites across the East Midlands. This view of the Stanton plant at Holwell gives a good impression of a typical ironworks just after the Great War.

H E L Tatham

Pye Hill Colliery, near Pye Bridge Station acquired a surplus BR Class 04 350HP shunting locomotive in the late Sixties, and for two more decades it remained in its original Brunswick Green livery. It is seen here in the colliery reception sidings alongside the main line

Authors Collection

A restored example of a standard RCH 7 plank open wagon operated by the Stanton Ironworks Company is on display at the National Railway Museum in York. This timber framed vehicle is typical of many thousands that operated out of collieries and ironworks in the Erewash Valley in the first half of the Twentieth Century

An early view of what is thought to be Long Eaton Station. Long Eaton was closed in the late 1960s, and the name taken by Sawley Junction.

H E L Tatham

One of Pye Hill's Sentinel diesel hydraulic shunters alongside the Erewash Valley line at Pye Bridge in about 1982. One of the original Midland buildings is in the background.

Author's Collection

This view of a double-headed southbound freight to the north of Trent Junction demonstrates the Midland Railway's small engine policy in action.

H E L Tatham

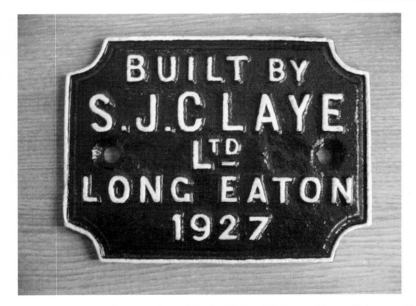

Claye's wagon works were located alongside the Midland Railway at Long Eaton, and just one of many railway connected companies that sprang up in the area.

A view over the drivers shoulder on a southbound DMU near Langley Mill in around 1970. The straight alignment is shown to good effect in this picture.

Ronald Askew

SUNCOAL BUILDINGS

G.N.R

LMS

BRIDGE
DATED
1861

D. ReRu
(15.6.11)

THE TO BABINGTON COLLY
SIDINGS D. ReRu (16.6.11)

LINE TO BROXTOWE
COLLY / BEWCASTLE LEVEL
CROSSING TO NEWCASTLE
COLLY D. ReRu (16.6.11)

WOLLATON HALL.
Nottinghamshire.

Wollaton Park 1812. This view was published in the Beauties of England and Wales, 1813. Sir Francis Willoughby began to build his new hall in 1580 and it was eight years before it was completed. Much of the land had already been enclosed, first in 1492 as a park for wild animals – deer and wild white cattle occupied the land and the bulls were hunted – and a further 100 acres in 1510

However the p
Wollaton Hall, t
actually two ha
How did this co

It was all to i
any woman – it
Elizabeth the F
loughby, who e
Robert Smyths

2.2 From Basford to Bennerley

In 1879 a cross country link was opened connecting the Midland's Mansfield line with its main line to St Pancras. Commencing at Basford Junction, the line travelled due west, cutting through the high land dividing the Leen and Erewash valleys at Watnall. From Kimberley, the line traversed the flat bottom of the Erewash Valley to join the main line at Bennerley. The line had no passenger service initially, but three years after, it opened intermediate stations at Watnall and Kimberley. These were modest single storey affairs constructed in local red brick and provided with small goods yards. Freight traffic was expected to be generated from connections to colliery yards and ironworks at Watnall and Bennerley, Watnall brickworks, the brewery at Kimberley and lime kilns on the north west outskirts of Bulwell.

The remains of the junction for Bennerley are viewed from the site of Basford Junction Signal Box in 1983. By this time the line was just a spur a few hundred yards long, and it disappeared altogether a few years later. The embankments of the GNR Derbyshire Extension are visible in the background, bridges 37 and 38 having been demolished a decade before.

Nottingham City Council

Unfortunately for the Midland, its expectations for the line were never realised. The predominantly rural route connected only a handful of population centres. The ones it did reach were already served by the GNR's Derbyshire Extension which offered a much more frequent service than anything the Midland could match.

There was little through freight on the line either, with all locally generated traffic heading for the Leen Valley line or the main line. Under combined pressure from the GNR and then the Nottingham Corporation's electric trams, passenger services were abandoned in 1917. Through goods traffic ceased in 1921 and the line was divided into two dead end branches serving Bennerley Colliery at the western end, and a singled freight branch to Kimberley at the east.

The abandoned bridge over Cinderhill Road is seen here in December 1963. This was the largest structure on the line and remained in use until 1954, when trains to Watnall Colliery finished. The piers and abutments were Bulwell Stone, and the deck was wrought iron.

Ronald Askew

Traffic on the eastern branch gradually dried up, and this section finally closed in 1954. Much of the track bed was redeveloped in the 1970s. Today a short length of overgrown trackbed near Sellers Wood and an abandoned single span occupational bridge alongside the M1 motorway are all that remain of this section.

Most of the central portion has also been reclaimed, as could be expected for such an early casualty. Opencast mining in post-war years eradicated much of the route in the Erewash Valley. Watnall Station yard was bought by the Air Ministry in the late thirties, and a regional command centre was constructed on the site.

Kimberley Station buildings have proved to be the most surprising survivor however, especially when it is considered how long they have been out of use.

The disused alignment at Sellers Wood is seen here in December 2005. Apart from this short section of overgrown embankment, nothing else remains of the line to the east of the motorway.

The M1 motorway bisects the route against bridge No 15, near Nuthall. This wrought iron-decked structure sits on Bulwell stone abutments, and has red brick jack arches between the beams. It carries a farm access and today stands sandwiched between unbroken fields and the motorway. The last train passed here in 1954 and today much of the route has been reclaimed for agricultural use.

Kimberley Station was purchased by the adjacent Kimberley Brewery after closure and used for many years as a social club. The buildings have had a chequered history since then, having several small but ill matching extensions added, and suffering fire damage and vandalism. The Social Club closed in the Nineties, and the building has stood derelict and boarded up since then. At the time of writing there are no slates on the roof and part of the structure is open to the elements.

The station yard was also purchased by the Brewery, and the goods yard area has never been redeveloped, remaining as an open space to the west of the station. The north of the site is still bounded by the large red brick retaining wall that the Midland Railway built to support the Brewery's land, and the parapets of the infilled bridge that carried Hardy Street across the railway can still be seen. To the west of the site, the eastern abutment of the bridge that once carried the line across the road to Eastwood also remains in position, although the west abutment and deck are long gone, along with the remainder of the formation heading towards Bennerley.

The old station site falls within the Kimberley Conservation Area, so it enjoys a limited amount of Planning Protection from the Local Authority, although it is not actually listed. Whether it is rescued and finds another use, or continues to deteriorate to the point where it cannot be saved remains to be seen.

It is remarkable that Kimberley Station should survive ninety years after closure. At the time of writing it had been boarded up for some years, and had lost its roof slates and some of its original chimney stacks. A great deal of original detail remained in place however.

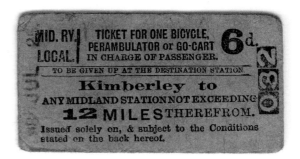

The early closure of the line to passengers makes tickets for the two stations very rare. This article ticket from Kimberley Station is for the conveyance of a bicycle or pram on the line.

Ian Askew Collection

The western spur of the Bennerley branch outlasted the other sections of line, surviving even the closure of Bennerley Ironworks, to be used by traffic for an opencast coal washing plant that was built on the site. At the time of writing, the rails are still in situ, but the line is not in active use.

A birds eye view of the western end of the Basford – Bennerley branch taken from Giltbrook Viaduct on April 12th 1968. A rake of redundant wagons can be seen in store in the distance.

Ronald Askew

● NOT ALL TRACKS LIFTED BETWEEN .
BENNERLEY COLLIERY + KIMBERLEY WEST
STATION + GOODS YARD ?? IN 1917 ??
D. GIBBS
(10. 12. 2013)

2.3 Radford Junction to Trowell

The branch from Radford to Trowell opened in 1875. It gave southbound traffic on the Midland main line with a more direct route into Nottingham than the tortuous route via Toton Yard and Trent Junction, and provided access to Trowell Moor, Newcastle and Wollaton Collieries. The line was barely five miles in length, and had no public stations along its route, although a simple halt was later provided for workmen's trains serving Wollaton Colliery.

The steelwork for Trowell Road bridge was fabricated at a Leicester iron foundry, and would have been transported to site by rail along the Erewash Valley line.

Trowell Road bridge as it exists today was built in 1909. This skew decked rivetted steel structure replaced an earlier masonry arch bridge. Until the 1960s a Midland Railway standard signal box stood just beyond the bridge on the left, facing the point where the Wollaton Colliery branch diverged. Today a supermarket occupies the former pit site.

Nottingham City Council

The route was double track throughout, and initially carried a substantial amount of traffic. Trowell Moor and Newcastle Collieries closed before the Second World War and Wollaton Colliery finished in 1965. The loss of this traffic and the run down of local services led BR to earmark the line for closure on several occasions. It eventually closed to traffic and was mothballed in the early Nineties, with all traffic being routed through Toton Yard. The line was granted a reprieve however and reopened a couple of years later. At the time of writing it is used primarily by Nottingham to Sheffield trains and services for the north west, together with the occasional freight movement.

Balloon Woods footbridge is one of the earlier structures on the line, and dates to its opening in 1875. When first built it provided access to clay pits, providing raw materials for local brickworks. The pipe bridge in front is a later addition.

Nottingham City Council

2.4 Pye Bridge to Kirkby

Pinxton signal box is a Type 2b Midland design, and dates from 1897. In December 2005 it was still equipped with 28 levers, the majority of which were still in use. The station stood on the far side of the level crossing, but no trace of this now remains.

The area between Pye Bridge and Kirkby in Ashfield saw the development of numerous collieries from the late Eighteenth Century onwards. Horse drawn tramways connected these with the canal network, but in 1847 the Midland Railway embarked on the construction of a standard gauge railway to tap into this coal traffic.

The route of the line was to be from a new junction on the Erewash Valley line, through Pinxton and on to Mansfield, joining the Midland's line up the Leen Valley at Kirkby Junction. A new junction station would be built at Pye Bridge, to replace Codnor Park Station to the south, and a single station would be provided on the new line itself at Pinxton & Selston.

The line opened to freight in 1850, and to passengers the following year. The line connected with the Leen Valley route to the north of Kirkby Station, so passenger trains from the Erewash Valley were unable to stop at the town.

The situation was remedied in 1892 when a new spur connected the two lines on the south side of Kirkby.

Coal traffic from the half dozen or so pits along the five mile route generated healthy returns, but passenger traffic was more sparse. Pinxton & Selston was closed to passengers by the LMS in 1947, but continued in use for workmen's trains until 1965.

The decimation of the Notts coalfield in the early Nineties saw a dramatic reduction in freight traffic, however sufficient remained to warrant the line's survival. Like many freight backwaters, little investment has been undertaken, and at the time of writing, Midland signal boxes survive at Sleights Sidings and Pinxton. A fine display of semaphore signals can still be seen at the latter location.

Many of the signals at Pinxton date from the steam era, and all are still wire-worked. Oil lamps have been replaced with electric operation, but otherwise this view taken in December 2005 could easily date from half a century earlier.

2.5 The Derbyshire Extension of the GNR

The Route Described

The first section GNR Derbyshire Extension opened in 1875. It ran from a triangular junction with the Ambergate's Grantham line at Colwick, skirting north around Nottingham's outer suburbs before turning west and heading for Derby.

The portion of the line between Colwick and Basford was known locally as the Back Line, and this is described in Volume One.

At Basford the line was crossed by the Great Central. When Nottingham Victoria opened in 1900, GNR services to Derby were diverted here from London Road. The trains now bypassed the eastern leg of the old GN line and using the more direct GC route, gained the Derbyshire Extension at Bagthorpe Junction to the east of Basford & Bulwell. This station was the third on the line, and of relative importance due to its connections with the GCR. Junctions were provided between both routes in each direction, and carriage sidings were constructed in the space between the two routes.

The Midland line along the Leen Valley was encountered a short distance west of Basford and Bulwell. To cross this, the GN built a steeply skewed wrought iron lattice girder bridge (No 37) with a span of 100 feet. Immediately following, a nine span red brick viaduct (No 38) took the line over the River Leen. A facing junction to the west connected with Cinderhill Colliery.

The fourth station at Kimberley was situated at the end of a deep cutting. Station Road crossed the line on a level crossing to the west of the platforms. The adjacent Main Street was lowered, crossing under the line by means of an underbridge (No 47).

Pushing into the Erewash Valley the line branched north (for Newthorpe, Eastwood and Pinxton) before reaching the last station in Nottinghamshire at Awsworth. To the west of this the line crossed into Derbyshire on a magnificent wrought iron trestle viaduct at Bennerley. This structure towered 50 feet above the River Erewash and crossed the Midland's Sheffield – Derby route. At over 500 yards long, it was one of the largest structures of its type, and one of the last viaducts to use wrought iron. By the end of the nineteenth century this material had been displaced in favour of steel for bridge construction.

After stopping at Ilkeston North, the line branched for Marlpool and Heanor (Gate) to the north, and Stanton Ironworks to the south before proceeding to West Hallam and Breadsall. The line finally reached Derby Friargate after a total journey of some 25 miles.

Bennerley Viaduct is seen here in 1981, viewed from its western end. The Midland Railway's Erewash Valley line can be seen passing beneath it, and the NCBs coal washing plant is just visible to the rear.

Traffic

The route chosen by the GNR around Nottingham's northern outskirts avoided the necessity of pushing through dense urban areas, reducing construction time and costs. It did not provide the most direct journey for Derby bound passengers, but it did provide freight with a direct route from the Nottinghamshire and Derbyshire coalfields to the expanding sidings at Colwick.

Moving coal was the Derbyshire Extensions primary business. Collieries along the network of lines in the Leen and Erewash valleys, together with those at Gedling and Cinderhill generated enormous volumes of traffic. Much of this coal traffic was routed through the yards at Colwick, and from there it was distributed across the country via the company's network. Coal was not the only commodity carried by the line. A string of ironworks sprang up along both Erewash and Leen valleys, and iron ore from quarries in the Vale of Belvoir supplied them by way of the GNR's Grantham line. Traffic was so considerable that Colwick sidings would evolve in time to become the largest facility of its kind in Europe. Even in its twilight years it remained the biggest yard in the region, and access to it was to play a part in the life and death of the Derbyshire Extension.

The Stations

Stations along the line were generally constructed to a standard design. This comprised a substantial two storey station house on the main platform, with a range of single storey structures attached, containing waiting rooms, booking offices and toilet facilities. The facing platform usually had a hipped roof timber-built waiting room to variations of a generic design that appears to have been used widely across the East Midlands.

Kimberley Station is probably the most intact survivor on the line. It is seen here in 2000, before it was partially stripped out. The site of the platforms is now a car park, and a nature trail extends east along the abandoned track bed.

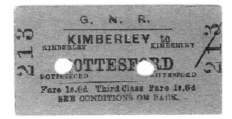

Third Class tickets for journeys from Kimberley and Awsworth stations dating from the Great Northern period.

Ian Askew Collection

The station at Basford & Bulwell (later renamed Basford North) differed from others on the line in being constructed from local Bulwell Stone, and sported some notably ornate chimney stacks. Train capacity was increased here by construction of a third platform face when the GCR arrived. Awsworth Station also differed from the other stations along the route but in a different way. Simple timber buildings provided rather basic passenger accommodation here, and the platforms were also wooden. This station was also of only a two on the route to be built without any goods yard facilities.

Ilkeston North, like Basford & Bulwell had an additional platform face. This was provided for local branch traffic. The island platform buildings were more substantial than other stations and constructed from local brick, but the main station buildings bore a family resemblence to others on the line.

Some civil engineering difficulties

Many structures on the Derbyshire Extension appear to have suffered maintenance problems during the life of the line, and some from a surprisingly early age. The Company's choice of an indifferent quality red brick for facing its structures, and poor attention to drainage detail caused rapid deterioration on many of the bridges. Mining subsidence was also particular difficulty and several bridges required complete renewal in LNER days, including ones at Gedling, Basford and Cinderhill. Deterioration of Mapperley Tunnel due to subsidence ultimately led to closure of the section of line from Basford to Colwick in 1960, and with it the direct link to Colwick Yards was lost.

All remaining traffic was diverted via the GC, and the line west of Bagthorpe Junction clung to life for a few more years. Closure of Derby Friargate in 1964 led to a withdrawal of passenger services, but limited freight services continued until these finished in May 1968 when the route through Nottingham Victoria was lost.

The line after closure

Most traces of the line within the built up areas of the City's suburbs have now vanished. Basford & Bulwell Station was swept away soon after the line closed, and many of the structures to the east of Cinderhill were demolished in the early Seventies.

Once clear of the Nottingham conurbation there are more tangible remains, including the substantially intact Kimberley Station, occupied for many years by the widow of the last Stationmaster. The original level crossing gates, platforms and lattice footbridge even managed to remain in situ until the mid Nineties. The building was refurbished internally in 2002, and sadly many original GNR fixtures and fittings were burned or scrapped by the builders. The next station at Awsworth was even less fortunate, being completely demolished and replaced by housing.

For more than thirty years, Kimberley Station remained pretty much as the track lifting gangs had left it. The platforms, footbridge, crossing gates, station buildings and weighbridge office all remained in situ, if somewhat overgrown. In the mid-Nineties much of this was cleared, to create a car park and nature walk.

Ian Askew

Kimberley Station is seen here in 2000. The ventilators on the roof were positioned above the toilet block. These were removed, and the building much altered as part of a residential development, a short while after the picture was taken.

Most of the GNR bridges in the Erewash valley area were completely demolished during the Seventies to accommodate major road developments. Odd abutments and parapet fragments survive however at locations around Kimberley and Awsworth, and two complete structures survive and are maintained in a serviceable condition.

The first is a concrete bridge carrying the M1 motorway over the line. This saw barely three years of actual use before the line closed, but it continues to be maintained in good order by the Highways Agency as part of the motorway infrastructure.

The second is Bennerley Viaduct. This wrought iron structure is one of only two of the type to survive nationally and the only completely intact example left. It is miraculous that it escaped demolition when the other major structures were removed in the 1970s and it now has listed status. Sadly this landmark has failed to find a new role, and is presently inaccessible to the public for reasons of safety. The approach embankments to the viaduct were removed during the Eighties, leaving it with an oddly stranded appearance standing isolated in the middle of the Erewash Valley.

Bridge No 44 at Nuthall was one of many occupational crossings of the route. Built with blue brick faced abutments and pilasters, it had a wrought iron deck. The central section of parapet appears to have been made of timber, a relatively unusual feature that the GNR seems to have adopted on several structures in the area. New Farm Lane over it is still used, but the cutting beneath has been filled for many years now.

flections: Nigel Mill took this view of Clumber Park. We are looking for photographs that convey the essence of the city or
unty or tell a news story. Please e-mail them to **pictures@nottinghampost.com** and include your telephone number.

The figures

Weather statistics for February 2014 (data taken from Andrew Shaw's weath station in Stapleford)
Mean monthly temperature: 5.8°C (1.7°C above the long-term norm)
Average daily maximum temperature: 8.7°C (1.7°C above the long-term norm)
Warmest day: 12.5°C, Februa 20
Average daily minimum temperature: 3.0°C (1.9°C above the long-term norm)
Coldest night: -1.3°C, Februa 10
Monthly precipitation: 51.4mm (109 per cent of long-term norm)
Monthly sunshine: 126% of normal

ggy scene: The Erewash Valley flooded at Bennerley Viaduct, between Ilkeston and Awsworth, on February 1, 2014

The M1 bridge was built over the line in 1965, barely three years before trains finished. The rock cutting beneath is now waterlogged and overgrown, the railway drainage having fallen into disrepair and in places buried.

Routes to nowhere:

Above : The abandoned cutting at Nuthall is seen here in 2006, flooded and overgrown.

Below : The empty trackbed stretching across the deck of Bennerley Viaduct is seen here in 1985. Although the formation had been abandoned some 17 years previously, the ballast is still surprisingly free of weeds.

Bridge 51 carried the line across the Erewash Canal and dated to the construction of the line in 1877. By the time it was photographed in 1981 this wrought iron structure was looking decidedly shabby and missing its brick newel posts. It was demolished two years later, and the approach embankments removed to leave no trace of the railway.

2.6 By GN to Pinxton

The Great Northern Railway's branch to Pinxton was constructed in 1875, diverging from the route of the Company's Derbyshire Extension at Awsworth. Oddly it was built before the main line was completed through to Derby. Consequently when it opened Pinxton marked the north-west extremity of the Company's interests in the area, and the terminus of the line from Colwick.

A junction was added at Awsworth two years later and the Derbyshire Extension pushed westwards to Derby and beyond. The line from Awsworth to Pinxton was effectively demoted to branch line status, although the large amount of traffic it generated ensured it would continue to be much more than a mere backwater.

Of double track throughout, the line incorporated some substantial civil engineering. Barely a hundred yards from Awsworth junction the line ran across one of the most impressive structures to be built in the County. Officially known as Bridge No 1 (Pinxton branch), this lofty structure was referred to locally as Forty Bridges. Built in local red brick, the viaduct measured some 1500 feet in length, and towered up to sixty feet above the Erewash Valley.

As its name suggested, the structure comprised 40 spans, two of which incorporated cottages built into the arches. Other notable features crossed by the structure included the Erewash canal, the Midland line from Basford, lines extending from Digby Colliery yard and a couple of local roads.

North of the viaduct the line reached Newthorpe & Greasley station. This was built along similar lines to other stations on the Derbyshire Extension, with the main buildings located on the up side of the line.

The next stop at Eastwood & Langley Mill was unusual in that it had a booking hall sitting above the tracks on the overbridge that carried Derby Road. Steps led to two facing platforms on the north side of the bridge. A range of single storey buildings at platform level included the stations north signal box, situated towards the far end of the Up platform. A similar layout was adopted a few years later in a several stations on the Leen Valley branch.

The Pinxton branch viaduct (Forty Bridges) is seen at distance from the Derbyshire Extension line at Awsworth in 1970. Demolition commenced shortly after this view was recorded, and today, no trace remains of this structure.

Ronald Askew

Eastwood & Langley Mill station was accessed from the far side of Derby Road bridge by two flights of steps. By 1982 the bridge was the only structure to remain on the southern portion of line. The remainder had been obliterated by construction of the A610 or buried beneath colliery spoil heaps.

Neill Fisher

X HEDGEROWS OF L.M.S. LEEN VALLEY JUNC.
TO NEWMALLEY JUNC RAILWAY LINE.
(THIS SECTION CLOSED IN 1921)
D.S

Heading north, the route crossed a maze of colliery lines on a multi span wrought iron overbridge before meeting up with the Midland Railway, which it paralleled for a further four miles. Both lines closely followed the River Erewash upstream as it traced out the County boundary.

The next station at Jacksdale was little more than a halt, with single storey timber buildings providing meagre accommodation. The unusual feature of this station however was its location, atop a 20 span red brick viaduct (bridge No 21). The platforms were accessed via a flight of steps with the booking Hall and Parcels Office built into two of the arches beneath.

A further halt was provided a mile further north at Pye Hill & Somercotes, with similar timber shelters to Jacksdale, but none of the idiosyncrasies of its southern neighbour.

Pinxton was not quite the end of the line. An end on junction with a freight only single line tapped additional colliery traffic from around the South Normanton area, pushing the GNR's direct influence to its northernmost limit in Derbyshire.

Passenger services lasted until January 1963 but progressively diminishing coal traffic continued until the line closed completely in 1966.

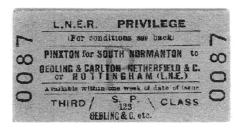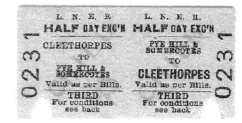

Tickets for travel from Pinxton and Pye Hill & Somercotes Stations issued during LNER days. The half day excursion was doubtless some lucky child's trip to the seaside!

Ian Askew Collection

The GNR terminus at Pinxton is seen here in August 1955. The buildings were identical to those used on the Derbyshire Extension, and at Newthorpe.

N(B)MRS / D R Morley

The final stop on the line was the terminus at Pinxton (South). This station was again built to the same general design as those of the Derbyshire Extension, but this time the platforms were offset from each other. A goods yard and locomotive facilities were provided, including a small shed, coaling stage and turntable.

Collieries generated most of the traffic on the line, and large private networks of colliery railways sprang up in the area. By the Eighties, few collieries remained open and the writing was on the wall for those that remained. Formerly Class 10 No D3619, NCB No D15 "Simon" is seen here crossing the A608 on the Moorgreen Colliery Railway on 25th April 1984.

Ian Askew

The final remains of Eastwood & Langley Mill Station are swept away for an extension of the A610 in 1982. The new road alignment can be seen in the distance.

Neill Fisher

NCB for opencast and waste tipping. Pinxton Station was sold to a plant hire company, and the site cleared. Today the only traces remaining of the railway are a few fragments of overgrown alignment just to the south of Pinxton. Of the lines covered by this book, few have disappeared as completely as the GNR branch to Pinxton.

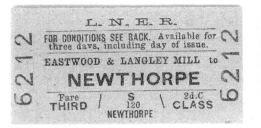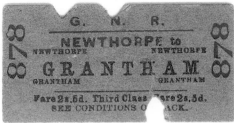

Tickets for journeys from Eastwood & Langley Mill, and Newthorpe stations dating from both LNER and GNR days.

Ian Askew Collection

Reclamation of the route commenced within a couple of years of closure. Forty Bridges was demolished in 1970, and three years afterwards, a new dual carriageway was constructed along the alignment of the railway, obliterating Newthorpe Station and virtually every trace of the route as far as Eastwood.

The new road terminated at the site of Eastwood & Langley Mill station, and for several years the former overbridge that once carried the booking hall stood isolated in the centre of an elevated roundabout. The trackbed to the north of here was converted to an industrial access road, but this was also eventually upgraded to dual carriageway in the Eighties, when the A610 was extended to bypass Langley Mill. Former sidings to the south of Eastwood & Langley Mill were acquired by a local Engineering company, together with the south signal box. This was demolished and the site cleared for construction of a new drawing office and car park in 1971. Even this was not to last however, with the company closing in the Nineties and a housing estate taking its place.

The station and viaduct at Jacksdale were demolished in 1974. The site of Pye Hill & Somercotes station and a sizeable slice of the formation were taken by the

This somewhat grainy view shows the northernmost extent of the line at Pinxton. The Midland Railway can be seen in the background and empty coaching stock is being stored in the yard.

N(B)MRS / D R Morley

3. The Lincoln Line

The railway from Nottingham to Lincoln was one of the first to be built by the newly formed Midland Railway. It was born out of the amalgamation of three separate companies in 1844, and in 1845 it obtained powers to construct the line. The route followed the line of the Trent Valley, so required few earthworks or bridges. This is evident from the remarkably short period of time required in which to build the line. It took just nine months from breaking ground to the first public train running, an achievement that seems incredible by today's standards.

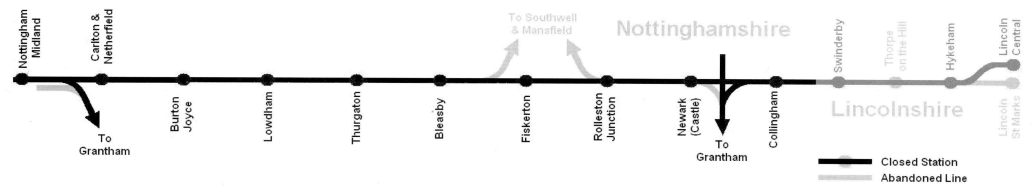

Above : Route map of the Nottingham – Lincoln line as it exists today. Junctions at Netherfield and Newark were constructed in the 1960s, although a junction had existed at the former location during the 1850s. The junctions at Rolleston and Fiskerton were abandoned in 1965 with the closure of the route to Mansfield.

Above : Sneinton Junction signal box was built in 1914, and controlled traffic entering the exchange sidings with the Great Northern. By 2005 it was reduced to the status of gate box, controlling Meadow Lane and Colwick Road crossings. The box is destined to be abolished under the Trent Resignalling proposals towards 2010.

The Lincoln line eventually had twelve intermediate stations, of which nine fell inside Nottinghamshire. Station buildings and crossing keeper's houses on the line were designed with considerable attention to detail, and appear to have been finished in three distinct architectural styles, each of which were popular in the early Nineteenth Century. An Italianate form was adopted at a number of buildings. Shallow-pitched fully hipped roofs had substantial overhangs supported by stone corbels, and windows and doorways were given semi-circular heads. These were frequently oversailed by stone pediments. Other structures had a Jacobean flavour, with flush eaves, heavy cornerstones and stone mullioned windows. The final style followed the Victorian fashion of a romanticised rural form. Steeply pitched roofs carried tall decorative chimneys and the gables were finished with ornately carved barge boards, giving a Tudor cottage like appearance. This style was reminiscent of many country estate gate houses of the period, perhaps suggesting why the Midland Railway chose it.

Whilst architectural style varied, constructional materials were generally consistent. Surprisingly yellow brick was used as the primary material, with the more readily available local red brick or stone only used in occasional cases. Slate was used as the primary roofing material.

Colwick Crossing Gatehouse dates from the opening of the line and was built in the Jacobean style, with attractive results. It is seen here in January 2005, and has benefited from sympathetic restoration work in recent years.

the town. The routes were eventually linked by a single track line for exchange traffic, which crossed the Newark branch of the River Trent on a wrought iron two span bridge to the west of the flat crossing.

An unidentified Fairburn Class 4 pilots a Midland 2P on a Lincoln train past Colwick Woods, adjacent to the GNR's Hall sidings on March 1st 1955.

N(B)MRS / D R Morley

Newark was the largest intermediate station on the route, and differed from others in being built to a classical style. The front of the station was colonnaded with a considerable amount of decorative stonework, and each end of the main building semi-circular in plan. The platforms were sheltered by glazed canopies supported by ornate cast iron columns finished with intricately cast capitols. Newark was a substantial market town, and in 1845 no other railway served it. Consequently the Midland Railway built a sizeable goods yard with ample facility for handling livestock. As industry began to develop in the town, connections to engineering works and maltings were added and additional sidings and warehousing built in the yard.

Despite the commodious facilities provided at Newark, the inaugural train did not actually stop there. This intentional snub arose from a dispute between the Midland Railway's management and local Town Officials!

The coming of the GNR to Newark in 1850 added a new dimension, with the introduction of a flat crossing where the two routes met on the north east side of

In the 1850s however, relations between the two companies were at the very best frosty. The rivalry between the two companies even led to the removal of the junction with the Ambergate, Boston & Eastern Junction line at Netherfield in 1857, after this route was taken over by the GNR (see Volume 1, Chapter 2).

In 1860 a branch was opened from Rolleston to Southwell, and a new station of that name built at the junction. This junction for this faced Newark, necessitating a reversal for direct trains to and from Nottingham.

In 1871 the Southwell branch was extended with a single line to Mansfield, and a new chord facing west gave a direct route for Nottingham trains. Coal traffic from the North Notts coalfield began to find its way along the route, travelling via Rolleston West Junction and the new chord to Fiskerton Junction en route to the yards at Toton.

Carlton & Netherfield Station was the first stop on the line, with staggered platforms to each side of a level crossing. The cottage style buildings on the Up platform are seen here in July 1955, and were demolished in the late Sixties.

N(B)MRS / D R Morley

By 1983 little original infrastructure remained, other than the platforms. A Swindon cross-country unit stands in the Down platform with a Lincoln train.

The late 1870s saw introduction of block signalling on the line, and from this time onwards standard Midland prefabricated timber signal cabins began appearing. By the start of the Twentieth Century, the line had reached maturity, and few infrastructure changes would take place until the advent of the Beeching Report.

Burton Joyce signal box, dating from around 1900, was unusual in being provided with a brick base. This was presumably because flooding had caused problems with the previous all timber structure. Seen here in 1982, the box and gates were removed shortly afterwards. The LNER gate lamp would have been fitted after the line transferred to the Eastern Region in 1958.

Probably the most noteworthy development in this time was the construction of Staythorpe power station to the west of Newark, just after the Second World War. This required prodigious quantities of coal which was provided by collieries that the Mansfield line served, together with those in the Leen Valley. Aside from the coal traffic, the line saw comparatively little freight. Engineering and agricultural products were generated at Newark, but the lack of any real heavy industry or mining elsewhere on the route meant that the line retained an essentially rural character for much of its life.

Passenger receipts were bolstered by race day specials serving Southwell racecourse, but the lack of large population centres along the route, with the arguable exception of Newark, meant that traffic would never be heavy.

It was lack of freight and falling passenger receipts that led to the line being recommended for closure in the Beeching Report (The Reshaping of British Railways) in 1963. This wide ranging report published by the British Railways Board also called for the cross-country route from Mansfield to Rolleston Junction / Fiskerton Junction to close, together with a number of other Midland routes in the area.

Facilities at Burton Joyce were fairly basic, with a modest single-storey booking hall on the end of the Down platform, and a timber shelter on the Up platform. A Lincoln to Derby train, comprising of a newly introduced 3 car DMU is seen here arriving at the station in 1958.

C A Hill

The Lincoln Route escaped closure, thanks in part to the opening of a second power station at Staythorpe in 1962, but there would be no reprieve for the Mansfield line, which closed in 1965. Thorpe on the Hill station also lost its services, being the only intermediate station on the Lincoln line to close. The Lincoln route was to undergo cost cutting and rationalisation in the following decade, with widespread removal of infrastructure and arguably little positive investment to attract the passengers back. The stations were reduced to unstaffed halts, and many lost their original buildings and with it their character.

Local freight traffic was abandoned, and yards were closed and their sidings were lifted.

Manually operated crossings gradually replaced with automatic barriers and CCTV cameras, allowing the closure of many signal boxes.

Steam made a return to Burton Joyce in February 1989, when preserved Stanier Class 5 No 44932 made a stop whilst on a special working. It is seen waiting in the Down platform.

In 1964 the Ambergate line junction at Netherfield was reinstated to facilitate the run down of the Great Northern route into Nottingham. Netherfield Junction signal box was added to the block circuits for the line and traffic to the west of the junction picked up considerably with the re-routing of Grantham trains.

In the early Seventies the line west of Netherfield Junction came under the Track Circuit Block control of the power box at Trent Junction. Colwick Crossing signal box was abolished and Sneinton Junction became a crossing box, losing its block post status. Sneinton Junction itself was lifted when the exchange yard and Great Northern goods facilities closed, allowing many of the levers in the old Midland box to be removed entirely. Semaphore signals gave way to colour lights on this western stretch of the line, and automated barriers replaced wooden gates.

Absolute Block signalling survived however on the line eastern reaches of the route. At the time of writing semaphore signals are still controlled by pre-grouping mechanical signal boxes at many locations. Block equipment has been modernised however, and the highly polished mahogany cased instruments of Midland days have been replaced by the standardised plastic cased equipment that BR introduced across the entire network.

hand operated timber crossing gates, oil lit semaphores and a Type 3A Midland signal box at rural Fiskerton.

It seems likely that these remaining pockets of traditional operation are destined to continue for some years to come, with Network Rail having no immediate plans for resignalling, other than maintenance renewals.

Despite closure of Staythorpe power station in the mid-Nineties, the Lincoln line today is not an exclusively passenger route. Freight has made a comeback in recent years, and now makes up a significant proportion of train movements. Immingham to Kingsbury oil trains make up the greater bulk of these, but aggregates and coal are also moved and the line is in use around the clock.

Passenger services are also well used, providing growing numbers of commuters with a more civilised alternative to the A46 and A612, both of which gridlock during peak hours. One is left to wonder what these roads would be like had Dr Beeching had his way in 1963 and the Lincoln line actually closed.

Above ; A friend of the Author poses for the camera at Lowdham in July 1982. This particular box (a Type 2b) was built in 1896 to replace an earlier structure. In 86 years, little had outwardly changed, and it is still in use at the time of writing.

Most signals date from LMS or early BR days, but a few are still mounted on Midland Railway pattern wooden posts, and some are even illuminated by long burning oil lamps, tended once a week by a lampman just as they were a century earlier.

Travelling the line today it is possible to see a complete spectrum of railway operation, ranging from the spartan 1970s style urban commuter halt at Carlton with its automated barriers, CCTV cameras and colour light signals, through to

The main buildings at Lowdham Station escaped demolition when it became an unstaffed in the late Sixties. When pictured in 1982 the station still had timber crossing gates and mechanical signalling. The yard had closed, but a siding still existed on the down side. Indeed apart from electric lights and a new Up platform shelter, little had outwardly changed since steam days.

Above : A Lincoln bound train pulls into Lowdham in 1958, in charge of Class 4 tank No 42331 of Nottingham Shed. Note the locomotive is carrying an incorrect headlamp code!

C A Hill

Opposite : The co-acting Down Home signal is seen here from the A6097 overbridge in 1985, together with the signal box and crossing gates. The second signal arm was necessitated by the presence of the road bridge, blocking the sight line. The use of lattice signal posts was relatively rare on LMS lines, being more favoured by the LNER.

John Mulhall

Two photographs taken at Thurgarton in March 1984. The view above shows a Class 120 DMU westbound. The original Up platform was out of use by this date, with a replacement provided beyond the crossing. The view below shows the signal box which dated from the early 1900s. It was demolished, together with the redundant platform shortly after the photograph was taken.

Above : A general view of the western approach to Thurgarton Station taken from the new Up platform in the summer of 1984. The box was classified as a type 3a design.

Below : Bleasby Station was built in the Italianate style. The main station house escaped demolition in the late Sixties, but every other vestige of the original station, including the platforms was swept away. New staggered concrete platforms replaced the originals.

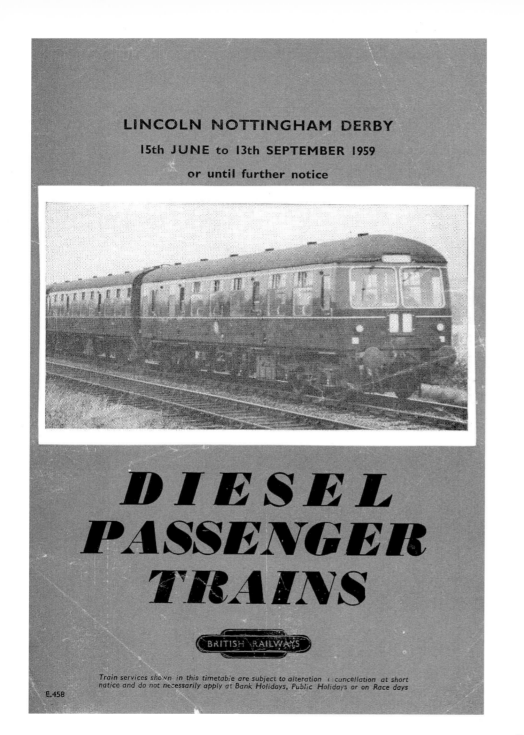

LINCOLN NOTTINGHAM DERBY

15th JUNE to 13th SEPTEMBER 1959

or until further notice

DIESEL PASSENGER TRAINS

BRITISH RAILWAYS

Train services shown in this timetable are subject to alteration or cancellation at short notice and do not necessarily apply at Bank Holidays, Public Holidays or on Race days

E.458

A Lincoln train arrives at Bleasby Station on 29th October 2005. The original station house can be seen on the left, but the Up platform has been relocated to the west of the crossing.

Bleasby Station survives today as a private residence and still carries the old Eastern Region colour scheme of green and cream that it was first given in 1958.

Opposite : Diesel services were introduced on the line in 1959 as a cost saving measure. It wasn't enough however to prevent it being recommended for closure in the Beeching Report .

Author's Collection

At Morton Crossing, the Midland provided a ground frame hut, for use when Fiskerton Junction box was closed out. By June 2005 it was out of use, but still intact

Fiskerton Junction box dates from 1915, but has recently had its windows and steps replaced. Surprisingly the crossing gates have also been recently renewed.

The close proximity of Fiskerton Junction box and Morton Crossing hut can be seen in this view. Today the box is just a block post, but is continuously manned.

Fiskerton Station approach, seen from the site of the former goods yard in 1986. The wooden post carrying the signal is a survivor from Midland Railway days.

The crossing gates have survived at Fiskerton Station. The crossing keeper operates these by hand, and is seen here preparing for the arrival of a train.

Fiskerton Station retains its 1902 signal cabin, but this is no longer a block post. It is seen here in 1986. The windows have since been changed, somewhat spoiling the cabins appearance.

After closure of the goods yard, Fiskerton Station gate box was reduced to only four working levers. Interestingly the original 1902 instrument shelf is still in place.

The junction at Rolleston closed in 1965. The station was reduced to an unstaffed halt, and the buildings demolished. Until the abolition of Rolleston Junction box, the signal post carried the station Up starter as well as Fiskerton Station distant. This view was taken in October 2005.

The Southwell branch platform was on the Down side of the station, and it still exists today, completely buried by undergrowth.

AVAILABLE OUTWARD AND RETURN ON DAY OF ISSUE IN EITHER DIRECTION BETWEEN ANY PAIR OF STATIONS FROM LINCOLN (ST. MARK'S) TO DERBY (MIDLAND) INCLUSIVE AT THE FARES SHOWN BELOW

Lincoln (St. Mark's)
1/4* Hykeham
2/6   1/8* Swinderby
3/4   2/7   1/0* Collingham
4/0   3/6   2/4* 1/10 Newark (Castle)
4/6   3/9   2/9   2/3   1/0   Rolleston Junction
4/9   3/9   3/3   2/9   1/3   4d*   Fiskerton
5/0   3/9   3/3   3/0   1/8   1/0* 8d*   Bleasby
5/3   4/0   3/6   3/3   2/0   1/4* 1/0* 8d*   Thurgarton
5/6   4/3   3/9   3/6   2/3   1/9   1/9   1/4* 1/0* Lowdham
5/9   4/9   4/0   3/9   2/9   2/0   2/0   1/7   1/6   1/0* Burton Joyce
6/0   5/3   4/6   4/3   3/0   2/3   2/2   2/0   1/10 1/6   8d*   Carlton & Netherfield
6/6   5/9   4/9   4/6   3/3   2/6   2/5   2/3   2/2   1/9   1/4   9d Nottingham (Mid.)
7/3   6/3   5/3   5/0   3/9   3/3   3/0   2/9   2/9   2/3   2/0 1/8 Beeston
7/6   6/6   5/6   5/3   4/0   3/6   3/3   3/0   3/0   2/6   2/3   2/0 Attenborough
7/9   6/9   5/9   5/6   4/6   4/0   3/9   3/6   3/6   3/0   2/9   2/6 Trent
8/0   7/0   6/0   5/9   4/9   4/3   4/0   3/9   3/9   3/3   3/0   2/9 Sawley Junction
8/3   7/3   6/3   6/0   5/0   4/6   4/3   4/0   4/0   3/6   3/3   3/0 Draycott & Breaston
8/6   7/6   6/6   6/3   5/3   4/9   4/6   4/3   4/3   3/9   3/6   3/3 Borrowash
8/9   8/0   7/0   6/9   5/9   5/3   4/9   4/9   4/9   4/3   4/0   3/6 Spondon
9/3   8/6   7/6   7/3   6/0   5/6   5/3   5/0   5/0   4/6   4/3   3/6 Derby

*Ordinary return fare available for return within three months

First class special cheap day tickets are also issued at approximately 50% over second class fares
Passengers may alight at a station short of destination in either direction upon surrender of the ticket
and commence the return journey from an intermediate station

DAY EXCURSIONS ON SUNDAYS

FROM	RETURN FARES SECOND CLASS TO				
	Matlock Bath	Matlock	Darley Dale	Miller's Dale	Buxton
	s. d.	s. d.	s. d.	s. d.	s. d.
Lincoln (St. Mark's)	11/9	12/–	12/3	15/–	15/6
Hykeham	11/–	11/3	11/6	14/3	14/9
Swinderby	10/–	10/3	10/6	13/3	13/9
Collingham	9/9	10/–	10/3	13/3	13/6
Newark (Castle)	8/6	8/9	9/–	11/9	12/3
Fiskerton	7/9	8/–	8/3	11/–	11/6
Bleasby	7/6	7/9	8/–	10/9	11/3
Thurgarton	7/6	7/9	8/–	10/9	11/3
Lowdham	7/–	7/3	7/6	10/3	10/9
Burton Joyce	6/9	7/–	7/3	10/–	10/6
Carlton & Netherfield ..	6/–	6/3	6/6	9/3	9/9

Enquire at stations for departure and return times

Published by British Railways (Eastern Region) BR35030/49

In 1958 it was possible to travel from Nottingham Midland to Rolleston Junction (return) for the equivalent of 12½ new pence!

An Ivatt Class 2 pulls into Southwell station with an SLS special in the late Fifties. All that remains of this scene today is the station house on the left.

C A Hill

Kirklington Station fared rather better than Southwell, and survives as a private residence. This portion of the track bed has been converted into a public right of way and is seen here in 1984.

Southwell Station closed to passengers in 1959, and the line closed entirely in 1965. Today the trackbed to the west of Southwell is a nature trail and walk.

In 1984 Farnsfield goods shed was still in good condition. When photographed it had just been repainted in Midland Railway colours, and was in care of the local authority. Sadly it was subjected to an arson attack a few years later, and today it is a gutted ruin.

Three views taken at Staythorpe Crossing in June 2005. This box was built by BR to an LMS design and opened in 1950 to handle traffic for Staythorpe Power Station. The prefabricated panels were substantially similar to those used by the Midland Railway, and would have been built in the Signal Workshops. At the time of the Author's visit, the box was still equipped largely as built. The sidings for Staythorpe Power Station were taken out of use late Nineties.

Below : An LNER pattern upper quadrant ground signal guarding the crossover at Staythorpe. Transfer of the line to the Eastern Region has resulted in a curious mixture of signalling equipment. In 2005 this signal was still oil-lit.

The next block post on the line from Staythorpe is Newark (Castle). The box here has outwardly changed little since construction and is the largest original Midland cabin to survive on the line.

Newark Station (renamed Newark Castle when the GNR arrived) was an imposing station when first built. Today it is a wine bar fronting an unstaffed halt.

Four Views here reflect five decades of freight working on the Lincoln Line and the changing scene in motive power terms:

Above : An unidentified Class 8F heads west past Colwick Woods and the adjacent GNR Hall sidings with an Up freight on 1st March 1955.

N(B)MRS / D R Morley

Below: An unidentified Class 31 heads west through Carlton Station in the summer of 1979 with an Engineers train.

Above : 47103 heads east through Carlton in March 1982 with an Immingham oil train.

Below : A Class 66 approaches Fiskerton Station with an aggregate working in December 2004.

LINCOLN NEWARK NOTTINGHAM DERBY

WEEKDAYS

	T		T	A		T	AB	JA	ET	S	T	ET	ST	T		SA	T	T	EV	SV	
	a.m.		a.m.	a.m.		a.m.	a.m.	a.m.	a.m.	a.m.	a.m.	a.m.	a.m.	p.m.		p.m.	p.m.	p.m.	p.m.	p.m.	p.m.
LINCOLN (St. Mark's) dep.	6 10	..	7 57	7 20	..	8 10	8 30	..	9 10	9 10	10 10	11 10	11 24	12 9	..	..	1 10	2 9	2 56	3 0	3 10
Hykeham	6 15	..	7 10	7 28	..	8 15	..	..	9 15	9 15	10 15	11 15	11 29	12 14	..	..	1 15	2 14	3 3	3 7	3 15
Swinderby	6 23	..	7 18	7 37	..	8 23	..	..	9 23	9 23	10 23	11 23	11 37	12 22	..	..	1 23	2 22	3 10	3 14	3 23
Collingham	6 27	..	7 22	7 43	..	8 27	..	..	9 27	9 27	10 27	11 27	11 42	12 26	..	..	1 27	2 26	3 15	3 19	3 27
NEWARK (Castle) arr.	6 35	..	7 30	7 50	..	8 35	8 51	..	9 35	9 35	10 35	11 35	11 49	12 34	..	..	1 35	2 34	3 22	3 26	3 35
" " dep.	6 36	..	7 31	7 53	..	8 36	8 56	9 15	9 36	9 36	10 36	11 36	11 52	12 35	..	1 10	1 36	2 36	3 25	3 29	3 36
Rolleston Junction	6 42	..	7 37	8 1	..	8 42	..	9 23	9 42	9 42	10 42	11 42	11 58	12 41	..	1 18	1 42	2 42	..	..	3 42
Fiskerton	6 44	..	7 39	8 4	..	8 44	9 4	9 26	9 44	9 44	10 44	11 44	12 0	12 43	..	1 21	1 44	2 44	3 33	3 37	3 44
Bleasby	6 47	..	7 42	8 9	..	8 47	..	9 30	9 47	9 47	10 47	11 47	12 3	12 46	..	1 25	1 47	2 47	..	..	3 47
Thurgarton	6 50	..	7 45	8 13	..	8 50	..	9 34	9 50	9 50	10 50	11 50	12 6	12 49	..	1 29	1 50	2 50	..	..	3 50
Lowdham	6 54	..	7 49	8 18	..	8 54	..	9 39	9 54	9 54	10 54	11 54	12 10	12 53	..	1 34	1 54	2 54	..	..	3 54
Burton Joyce	6 59	..	7 54	8 24	..	8 59	..	9 44	9 59	9 59	10 59	11 59	12 15	12 58	..	1 39	1 59	2 59	..	..	3 59
Carlton and Netherfield (for Gedling and Colwick)	7 3	..	7 58	8 30	..	9 3	..	9 49	10 3	10 3	11 3	12 3	12 19	1 2	..	1 44	2 3	3 3	..	..	4 3
NOTTINGHAM (Midland) arr.	7 9	..	8 4	8 36	..	9 9	9 21	9 55	10 9	10 9	11 9	12 9	12 25	1 8	..	1 50	2 9	3 9	3 51	3 54	4 9
DERBY (Midland) arr.	7 45	..	8 51	9 34	..	9 48	..	10 48	10 48	10 58	11 47	12 45	1 2	1 45	..	2 49	2K 51	3 46	4 33	4 33	..

WEEKDAYS (contd.)

	JA	T	T	E	T	T		AC	T	T	
	p.m.	p.m.	p.m.	p.m.	p.m.	p.m.		p.m.	p.m.	p.m.	
LINCOLN (St. Mark's) dep.	..	4 b 12	5 10	..	6 10	7 13	..	8 1	8 17	9 10	..
Hykeham	..	4 b 17	5 15	..	6 15	..	..	..	8 22	9 15	..
Swinderby	..	4 b 25	5 23	..	6 23	..	..	..	8 30	9 23	..
Collingham	..	4 b 29	5 27	..	6 27	7 27	..	..	8 34	9 27	..
NEWARK (Castle) arr.	..	4 b 37	5 35	..	6 35	7 35	..	8 22	8 42	9 35	..
" " dep.	4 10	4 b 38	5 36	5 55	6 36	7 36	..	8 31	8 43	9 36	..
Rolleston Junction	4 18	4 b 44	5 42	6 1	6 42	7 42	..	8 38	8 49	9 42	..
Fiskerton	4 21	4 b 46	5 44	6 3	6 44	7 44	..	..	8 51	9 44	..
Bleasby	4 25	4 b 49	5 47	6 6	6 47	7 47	..	..	8 54	9 47	..
Thurgarton	4 29	4 b 52	5 50	6 9	6 50	7 50	..	..	8 57	9 50	..
Lowdham	4 34	4 b 56	5 54	6 13	6 54	7 54	..	..	9 1	9 54	..
Burton Joyce	4 39	5 b 1	5 59	6 18	6 59	7 59	..	..	9 6	9 59	..
Carlton and Netherfield (for Gedling and Colwick)	4 45	5 b 5	6 3	6 22	7 3	8 3	..	..	9 10	10 3	..
NOTTINGHAM (Midland) arr.	4 55	5 b 11	6 9	6 28	7 9	8 9	..	8 56	9 17	10 9	..
DERBY (Midland) arr.	..	5 59	6 51	..	7 50	8 48	..	9 37	9 58	10 43	..

SUNDAYS

	T	AD	T	U		T	T	T	AZ	T
	a.m.	a.m.	a.m.	p.m.		p.m.	p.m.	p.m.	p.m.	p.m.
LINCOLN (St. Mark's) dep.	6 45	8 30	10 30	12 30	..	2 30	4 45	6 32	8 0	9 38
Hykeham	6 50	8 37	10 35	12 35	..	2 35	4 50	6 37	..	9 43
Swinderby	6 58	8 45	10 43	12 43	..	2 43	4 58	6 45	..	9 51
Collingham	7 2	8 50	10 47	12 47	..	2 47	5 2	6 49	8 16	9 55
NEWARK (Castle) arr.	7 10	8 57	10 55	12 55	..	2 55	5 10	6 57	8 23	10 3
" " dep.	7 11	9 1	10 56	12 56	..	2 56	5 11	6 58	8 30	10 4
Rolleston Junction	7 17	9 9	11 2	1 2	..	3 2	5 17	7 4	8 39	10 10
Fiskerton	7 21	9 13	11 6	1 6	..	3 6	5 21	7 8	..	10 14
Bleasby	7 23	9 15	11 8	1 8	..	3 8	5 23	7 10	..	10 16
Thurgarton	7 24	9 16	11 9	1 9	..	3 9	5 24	7 11	..	10 17
Lowdham	7 28	9 20	11 13	1 13	..	3 13	5 28	7 15	..	10 21
Burton Joyce	7 32	9 25	11 17	1 17	..	3 17	5 32	7 19	..	10 25
Carlton and Netherfield (for Gedling and Colwick)	7 36	9 30	11 21	1 21	..	3 21	5 36	7 24	..	10 29
NOTTINGHAM (Midland) arr.	7 43	9 36	11 28	1 28	..	3 28	5 43	7 31	8 56	10 36
DERBY (Midland) arr.	8 19	10 25	12 8	2d 37	..	4 20	6 29	8 19	9 37	11 19

A—Steam train   B—Through carriages Cleethorpes (depart 7.0 a.m.) to Birmingham (arr. 1113 a.m.) (to Bournemouth on Saturdays arr. 4.48 p.m.)   C—Through carriages Lincoln to Tamworth (arr. 10.23 p.m.)   D—Through carriages Lincoln to Buxton (arr. 12.15 p.m.)   d—Change at Trent   E—Except Saturdays.   J—Except Saturdays. Does not run 23rd July to 10th September inclusive.   K—On Saturdays arrives 2.49 p.m.   S—Saturdays only   T—Through train from Lincoln to Derby.   U—Through train Lincoln to Leicester (London Road) (arr. 2.29 p.m.)   V—Through train Lincoln to Derby (steam train)   Z—Through carriages Lincoln to Birmingham (arr. 11.12 p.m.)   b—On Saturdays runs 2 minutes later

4.0 Railways of the Leen Valley

Rising at Robin Hood's Chair near Kirkby-in-Ashfield the Leen flows south to Nottingham, before joining the Trent to the east of Trent Bridge. The history of the Leen valley has been shaped over the last two centuries by the coal industry. The bedding planes of the underlying rock strata in the region tilt to the east, and coal measures emerge in the broad shallow valleys of the Rivers Leen and Erewash. Coal has been dug here in small quantities since medieval times, but commercial collieries first started to appear at the end of the Eighteenth Century. By the close of the Nineteenth Century nearly a dozen major pits and numerous iron foundries were sited close to the Leen, served by three independent railway companies, each fighting to secure its own share of this lucrative traffic.

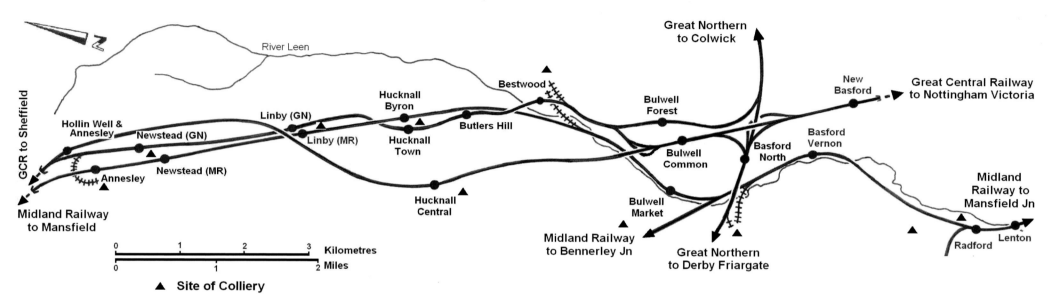

Railway map of the Leen Valley corridor Circa 1900

The plan above is abstracted from a contemporary map and shows the network at its zenith, at around the turn of the century. A further colliery branch to Calverton would be added after the Second World War, but by this time passenger services were in decline and many stations had closed. Station names shown are the ones in use at closure.

The Leen Valley eventually boasted the densest concentration of lines in the County, including privately owned colliery branches as well as through routes built by the principal railway companies. Eventually some nineteen stations were built between Kirkby and the city outskirts, including five sited within fifty yards of the River Leen itself.

The as the Twentieth Century progressed, the fortunes of the area went into decline. The economic hardships of the Thirties led to a number of station closures. The Beeching era saw duplicate routes axed and a total loss of the

remaining passenger services. Two decades later the decimation of the Nottinghamshire coalfield threatened complete disappearance of railways. The final freight operations in the area were the removal of coal recovered from Calverton Colliery spoil heaps, and this had finished by 1995.

Survival and ultimate regeneration of the remaining Midland route came in the Nineties, when Local Authorities led a scheme in partnership with British Rail to reinstate the railway through to Mansfield and reintroduce passenger services.

Today the "Robin Hood Line" has been augmented by a light rail link to Hucknall. This resulting combination of rail transport in the Leen Valley has become in important mode of transport for commuters and shoppers living to the north of Nottingham.

4.1 The Midland Railway in the Leen Valley

Whilst horse drawn wagon ways were in existence in the area at the start of the nineteenth century, the first main-line railway company didn't arrive on the scene until 1849.

The Midland Railway constructed its line from Mansfield Junction on the old Midland Counties line, a mile to the west of Nottingham, to a terminus at Mansfield, some fifteen miles to the north. With no other main line railways in the vicinity the Midland was able to take the easiest route, avoiding building major structures and closely following the River Leen almost to Kirkby, before diving through the Robin Hood Hills in a 250yd tunnel and striking north-west to Mansfield.

Intermediate stations were built at Lenton, Radford, Basford, Bulwell, Hucknall, Linby, Newstead, Annesley, Kirkby and Sutton. They generally followed the formula of facing platforms, with a two storey station house / booking hall on one side, a single storey shelter on the other, and access between platforms being taken via a level crossing.

An unidentified Class 8F is given a clear road through Radford Junction with a southbound loaded coal train in the winter of 1962.

C A Hill

Before the construction of Bobbers Mill Bridge in the 1930s, Nuthall Road crossed the Leen Valley line by a level crossing, situated immediately north of the sidings for Radford Colliery. The crossing and colliery are long gone, but the crossing keepers cottage survives, albeit in a ruinous state, on adjacent industrial land. Photographed in December 2005, it is almost certainly the oldest surviving structure associated with the line.

You have been warned! Radford Colliery sidings, 1958.

C A Hill

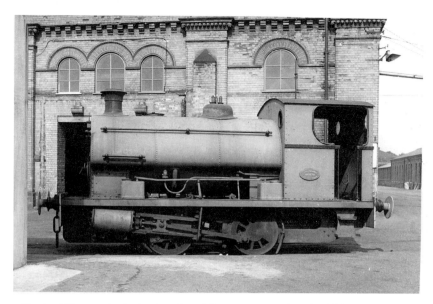

Basford Gas works had extensive sidings connected to the Midland Railway and operated several saddle tanks. Peckett Works No 1879 is seen here in 1966.

C A Hill

Ex Midland Class 2F No 58175 stands in Radford Yard in 1957. The 16A shedplate reveals that this is a Nottingham based engine.

C A Hill

Basford Vernon Station is seen from Church Street bridge (No 11) in 1955. The signal box is an LMS design, and replaced an earlier Midland box. It is relatively unusual in having a brick base. The track appears to be freshly ballasted.

C A Hill

A Class 4 tank is seen from the landing of bridge 11B, passing through Basford Vernon with a Mansfield train in 1962. Passenger services finished two years later.

C A Hill

The remains of Basford Vernon Up platform shelter are seen here in 1996 still in situ, albeit under a tangle of undergrowth.

The small station at Newstead differed from others on the line, and was built privately for the exclusive use of the owner of nearby Newstead Abbey.

As the line developed, so did the stations. Footbridge provision was made at several stations as traffic grew heavier, and level crossings gave way to overbridges at the busier stations serving the new suburbs of Lenton, Radford and Bulwell. A branch railway was constructed to Bestwood in 1873 serving the colliery and foundry, and in the same year Linby station was rebuilt with staggered platforms to accommodate sidings for the new colliery there. Further colliery connections were built at Hucknall, Newstead, Annesley and Kirkby, and in 1877 the private branch to Cinderhill colliery was purchased. Five years later, the Midland bought Newstead Station, and rebuilt it, allowing it to appear in the public timetable.

The expansion and development of Nottingham led to the construction of a series of gasworks by the City Corporation, including one at Basford. Gas was generated from coal, so a rail connection and yards were built to handle this new traffic. As traffic increased, changes were made to the line. The need to improve access to Hucknall No 2 Colliery and remove a busy level crossing led in 1895 to demolition of the original Hucknall station and realignment of Wigwam Road.

A new island-platform station was built a couple of hundred yards north of the original, with access from an overbridge in a style to be echoed later on by the Great Central Railway.

Junctions were constructed at Radford in 1875 and Basford in 1880 for branches to Trowell and Bennerley respectively, allowing access to the Erewash Valley without the need for travelling via Trent Junction. Early patronage was healthy, and revenues were sufficient to warrant extending the line north to Worksop in 1875. This golden period would be short lived however, with competition arriving in 1882 in the form of the Great Northern Railway.

Bulwell Market and Basford Vernon both closed to passengers on 10th October 1964.

Geoff Brain Collection

A third line arrived in 1899 when the Great Central opened, further eroding traffic that the Midland had previously monopolised. The Nottingham Corporation's electric trams brought additional competition from 1901, and contributed towards the premature demise of Lenton station in 1911. Through traffic over the Bennerley branch also finished early, when the branch from Basford Junction was reduced to a severed spur terminating at Watnall from 1915 (see Chapter 2).

Through the first half of the Twentieth Century local companies like John Players and Raleigh brought diversity to freight traffic on the line. Coal traffic was boosted in 1952 when a new colliery was sunk at Calverton, and a branch railway connected to the Midland at a point immediately north of the existing junction for Bestwood Colliery. A new signal box was provided at Bestwood Junction and the sidings were relayed and expanded.

The site of Basford Vernon Station in 1996. The platforms lay beyond the footbridge (No 11B) and the remains of the up platform and waiting room are still beneath the brambles. The goods shed to the right, was demolished along with the footbridge in 2002, to make way for the NET.

Despite heavy freight traffic, falling passenger revenues and increasing running costs in the post war years took their toll. The Beeching Report of 1963 targeted the line and passenger services were withdrawn the following year. In 1968 the line was closed completely from Annesley to Kirkby, leaving just the southern section open for coal traffic.

The closed section was cleared promptly, and part of the former railway alignment passed into ownership of the National Coal Board, allowing coal to be mined from the panel beneath the route. The cuttings on this section, together with Kirkby Tunnel, were filled with colliery spoil, whilst the approach embankment to the south of the tunnel was completely removed. The closed stations were demolished and soon there was little to show in some areas, that the railway had ever existed.

The Midland Type 4a box at Lincoln St Crossing was built in 1916 and is seen here in 1996. It was the last survivor on the line, being removed in 2002 during construction of the NET.

Examples of tickets from the final years of passenger services to Hucknall Byron Station.

Geoff Brain Collection

Bridge 15A to the south of Lincoln Street Crossing is the last original Midland footbridge on the line. Major repairs were carried out to this bridge in 2006, having been closed for two years due to its dangerous condition. It is seen in October 1996.

Basford Junction seen here in the early 1980s. By this time the Signal Box had been replaced by a ground frame, and the writing was on the wall for the Cinderhill Branch. The line paralleling the main line led to the long defunct Bennerley Branch, by now reduced to a spur barely 500 yards long.

Nottingham City Council

An unidentified Class 47 is seen running light engine past Lincoln Street box in 1989. The engine, gas lamp and palisade fencing are now long gone. The Midland Railway signal box was moved to a contractors training facility at Leicester after abolition.

Neill Fisher

The two way junction at Basford seen in the early 1980s. The main line is to the right, terminating by this time at Newstead. The single line to the left ran to Cinderhill Colliery, and the single line ahead once continued to Bennerley.

Nottingham City Council

The single track branch to Cinderhill crossed the River Leen on a three span structure (Bridge No 1). This bridge was rebuilt by the LMS and patched by BR, By 1982 it was deteriorating and this accelerated once the line was completely abandoned. In around 1999 it was severely damaged when a stolen car rammed the parapets and pushed them into the river. The bridge was replaced altogether in 2003 when the Cinderhill spur of NET was built along the old branch.

Nottingham City Council

The bridge beneath Cinderhill road spanned two separate branches. The connection to the Midland passed beneath the left arch and the GN connection passed beneath the right one. The bridge was constructed with the arrival of the GNR, and was classified as a GN structure. This view has changed somewhat with the construction of NET, and is now adjacent to the Cinderhill tramstop.

The end of Cinderhill Colliery Branch, seen in July 1984. Production has ceased and track recovery is underway. The redundant pit head gear is visible in the distance.

Nottingham City Council

Bridge No 17A to the south of Bulwell Market Station is seen here in October 1996. The bridge, together with the Up Distant for Lincoln Street Crossing were both removed in 2002.

An unidentified Fairburn Class 4 tank stands at Bulwell Market with a Worksop to Nottingham train on the final day of passenger services. 10th October 1964.

Ronald Askew

Three years after closure to passengers in May 1967 track relaying was undertaken, as this view taken from Highbury Vale at Bulwell shows. The tracked plant indicates that substantial work was undertaken to the formation before new panels were placed.

Ronald Askew

Fairburn Class 4 No 42218 is seen at Bulwell Market with a Worksop train on 10th October 1964. The station was demolished not long after closure.

Ronald Askew

To the north of Bulwell Forest Crossing, the Midland was crossed over by the Great Central's London Extension. The viaduct was classified on the Midland route as bridge 17C. The GCR had been out of use for more than 15 years when photographed here in 1981. The viaduct was demolished in 1989 to make way for a retail park

A panoramic view of Bestwood Park Junction approaches on 6th April 1981 reveals a pair of Class 20s light engine, on the outlet road from Betwood Sidings beneath Bridge No 17. The co-acting signal on the tall lattice post was typical of those installed on the LMS and latterly London Midland Region of BR, where a bridge deck obscured forward visibility. The bridge was built in the late 'thirties, by the Highway Authority to improve the road alignment and replace the narrower Bridge 19 that stood immediately to the north. The River Leen can be seen passing under the nearest span. Today the middle span is occupied by NET. The road embankment was built over the one time location of a well and watering hole for cattle that was known locally as the Bull Well, and which gave the area its name.

Nottingham City Council

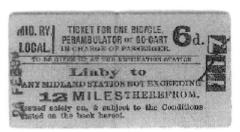

Tickets for journeys from stations on the Midland's Leen Valley line, dating from BR, LMS and MR days.

Ian Askew Collection

A pair of Class 20s head a southbound coal train out of Bestwood Sidings onto the main line in July 1980. The photograph was taken with an elderly Kodak Brownie. The Author stood on his bike saddle to take the shot over the parapet of Moorbridge!

The Calverton Colliery branch was completed in 1953. Former Lancashire & Yorkshire No 11257 is seen here in Contractors service during the construction of sidings at Calverton.

C A Hill

Bestwood Park Junction Signal Box, photographed during a heavy rain shower on 20th October 1996. This signal box was demolished to accommodate the construction of Moorbridge NET stop in 2002.

Stanier 8F No 48316 is seen on the Calverton Colliery branch in the winter of 1962 with a train of empties. Steam traction was extremely rare on the branch, and this appears, to the Authors knowledge to have been the only such working to be photographed.

Ronald Askew

Calverton Colliery remained open until 1998, and was the last source of coal traffic on the Leen Valley Route. A pair of Class 20s are seen here drawing an MGR train through the rapid loading bunker at Calverton on 17th March 1988.

Ian Askew

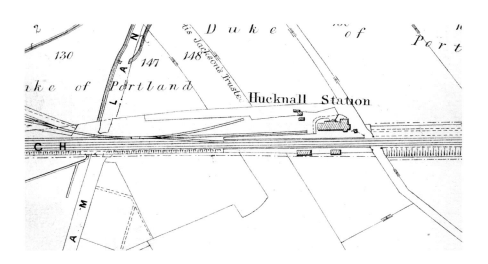

The Original Midland Railway Station at Hucknall as recorded on a GNR land plan of 1880. The station was reconstructed two decades later with a single island platform. Photographs of this original station are needless to say extremely scarce.

After the closure of Bestwood sidings the line north was rationalised. Beyond here it was singled. The junction for Calverton Colliery was located to Bestwood. Consequently two single track branches ran for half a mile on opposite sides of the formation. Byles & Whyles Occupational Crossing is seen here in 1996, to the north of Bestwood Park.

An unusual reminder of the Midland Railway was tucked away by allotments in Hucknall for many years. This Clayton 57' compartment third had been grounded and converted into a bungalow. The allotments have subsequently been cleared for development.

By 1983 Linby Station had been closed two decades. The colliery had closed and this section of line was mothballed. The platforms, signalling and station signal box still existed, but no trains ran here and the future looked bleak. The signal box controlled the north entry to the colliery sidings and appears to have been extended at some stage in its life.

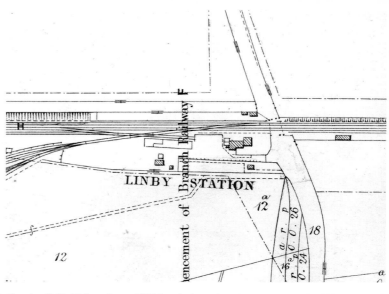

Linby Station in 1880. Taken from GNR land plans for the construction of its own branch, the drawing shows the station after reconstruction with staggered platforms. The main station buildings are now remote from either platform.

This 1962 view captures all three routes at Linby. A Class 47 heads a York-Bournemouth express on the GCR. It has just crossed the GNR line and is about to cross over the Midland, immediately north of Linby Station.

Ronald Askew

In May 1895 Queen Victoria was still on the throne, the Great Central Railway had yet to be built and a Third Class Single from Nottingham to Worksop via the Midland Railway Company's Leen Valley Line cost the equivalent of 11 new pence!

Ian Askew Collection

4.2 The Great Northern in the Leen Valley

In 1875 the GNR opened its Derbyshire Extension, giving it a platform from which to launch branches along the Leen and Erewash valleys to gain access to the lucrative coal fields.

Parliamentary powers were obtained for the Leen Valley line in 1880, and within two years construction was complete. The line diverged from the Derbyshire Extension at Leen Valley Junction, a mile to the west of Daybrook Station. This double track line required more substantial earthworks than its Midland rival, which had been able to closely follow the river. The largest structure on the line was provided where two routes crossed near to Bestwood. Bridge 12 comprised three wrought iron steeply skewed spans of 26' apiece carrying the GN line over the Midland.

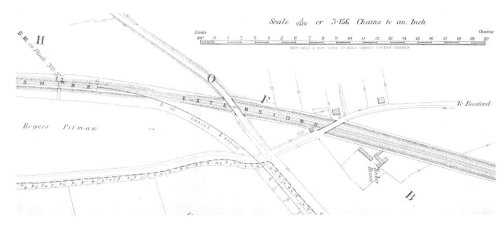

Leen Valley junction was constructed approximately 10 chains to the east of Hucknall Road overbridge (Bridge No 33). The indicative line above was prepared in 1880 to support the Bill for construction of the new line. The Derbyshire extension was just five years old, and it would be many decades before the suburban sprawl would reach here. Sidings were constructed to the east of the new junction as part of the works for the new line and bridge 32 was extended to accommodate the wider formation.

Author's Collection

Stations were provided at Bulwell Forest, Bestwood, Butlers Hill, Hucknall, Linby and Newstead. Expenditure on these was modest compared with the Derbyshire Extension, with provision comprising little more than a couple of timber platforms at several locations. Passengers were not however the company's motivation in building the line, with coal traffic being at the top of the agenda. The largest station at Hucknall Town, was a plain red brick affair accessed from an overbridge, located a short distance from the Midland's station and adjacent to Hucknall No 2 Colliery. Linby was also similarly constructed, but on a smaller scale.

Accesses were built to collieries at Bestwood, Hucknall, Linby, Newstead and Annesley. The colliery here initially marked the northern terminus of the line, which turned through 270 degrees in a tight 10 chain radius to enter the site.

Arnold Road overbridge seen here in 1981 was constructed by the LNER to replace an earlier structure. Immediately north of Leen Valley Junction, it was the first bridge on the route, and is today one of only a handful of structures to survive.

Nottingham City Council

The line may have been built without frills, but one notable exception was the overbridge crossing the carriage road into Newstead Abbey. At the insistence of the landowner, the structure was built with ornamental spandrels to disguise the wrought iron beams and cast iron balustraded parapets. The masonry was also finished with greater attention to detail than had been employed elsewhere, with limestone used as the primary material.

Other structures along the route were more mundane, typically being built in red brick, with wrought iron beams used for bridge decks and lattice girder through decks for footbridges.
Passenger traffic was not intensive, but freight workings proved lucrative. The GNR was well placed to route coal trains to its extensive yard at Colwick via the Derbyshire Extension, and from there across the entire network. An extensive wagon works sprang up by the station at Bulwell Forest, built by William Rigley who owned a local colliery engineering business.

For more than sixty years wagons and mining equipment would be built and repaired here for the collieries of the Leen Valley and further afield. The works eventually expanded to occupy 30 acres, and diversified into general engineering, with a second plant at Rugby.

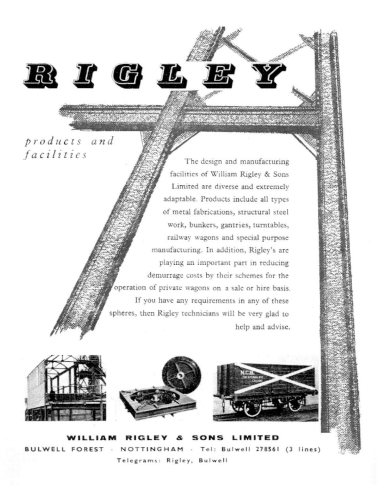

products and facilities

The design and manufacturing facilities of William Rigley & Sons Limited are diverse and extremely adaptable. Products include all types of metal fabrications, structural steel work, bunkers, gantries, turntables, railway wagons and special purpose manufacturing. In addition, Rigley's are playing an important part in reducing demurrage costs by their schemes for the operation of private wagons on a sale or hire basis. If you have any requirements in any of these spheres, then Rigley technicians will be very glad to help and advise.

WILLIAM RIGLEY & SONS LIMITED
BULWELL FOREST · NOTTINGHAM · Tel: Bulwell 278561 (3 lines)
Telegrams: Rigley, Bulwell

1950s Advert for Rigley's Wagon Works at Bulwell Forest

Author's Collection

The GN line was extended north in 1890, when the Manchester, Sheffield and Lincolnshire Railway reached Annesley. The MS&L and GN shared construction costs of tunnelling under the Robin Hood Hills, which gained the former access to the Leen valley coalfield, and the latter an economical way of pushing their line further north. The GN eventually reached Langwith Junction on the LD&ECR, taking in Kirkby in Ashfield, Sutton, Pleasley and Shirebrook on the way.

The final development of the route came in 1900, with the opening of a twin track connection to the Great Central's newly built London Extension at Bulwell North Junction. This link required two overbridges. An occupational bridge with a 20' span steel beam deck provided access to Bulwell Common, and Hucknall Road was spanned by a skewed steel truss of 40' span. The masonry was faced with Staffordshire brindled engineering bricks, in common with the structures of the Great Central.

By the 1960s wagon manufacture was in decline, and Rigleys began to undertake other types of work. This included breaking steam locomotives withdrawn from Colwick. A Class 02 is seen here in the sidings at Leen Valley junction in 1964 awaiting its final journey.

C A Hill

Passenger revenues were always modest, and in 1931 the LNER withdrew the remaining services, with an alternative service being offered on the GC route. The closed stations were maintained in serviceable order however, and continued to be used by the daily workmen's train. This service was known colloquially as the Annesley Dido, on account that it ran day in day out.

In 1958 the route was transferred to London Midland Region control, rendering it redundant as a duplicate of the old Midland line.

Withdrawn O2 freight engines are seen awaiting scrapping at Rigleys works in 1964. Bulwell Forest Signal box can be seen in the background.

Ronald Askew

Closure of Mapperley Tunnel in 1960 severed the direct route to the distribution yards at Colwick. Initially traffic was routed via Bulwell North Junction and the GCR, to Weekday Cross and back along the GN route to Colwick. The run down of the GCR and of Colwick Yards meant however a progressive transfer of traffic to the Midland and the yards at Toton. The last section of the line closed completely in 1968. The only fragment to remain was a mile long stub at Kirkby serving an industrial site.

The wrought iron spans of Bridge 12 were removed shortly after the line closed, and the steel bridge across Hucknall Road on the GC link was removed in around 1972.

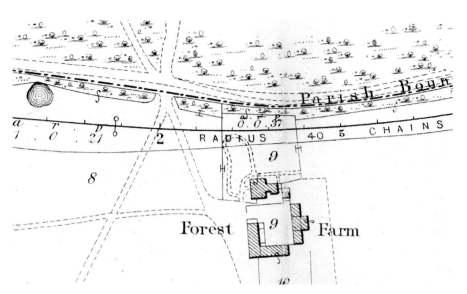

Rigley's Wagon Works took land formerly occupied by Forest Farm. The GNR took a considerable slice of farmland with the construction of the line, and its arrival marked a shift in the local economy from agriculture to industry.

Access to Bulwell Rise Farm was provided by Bridge No 4, seen here in 1984. When the area was redeveloped in the 1970s, a breach was made in the embankment for the construction of Bestwood Park Drive. Bridge 4 was kept, and the footway routed through it. The bridge was demolished in the early 1990s partly because of anti social behaviour problems in the area.

The route from Linby to Annesley was taken over by the NCB, who built a mechanical conveyor on the trackbed. For another twenty years this continued to move vast quantities of material, before the coal industry in the area closed down. Reclamation and landscaping subsequently removed much of the route, although a few sections still remain. Nottingham City Council converted the trackbed into a walkway alongside the A611, and a curious survivor can be found along the stretch south of Bestwood Park Drive in the form of a concrete post for a GNR somersault signal for the approach to Bulwell Forest. It remains in position on the Up side of the trackbed, almost completely obscured by tree growth. The ornate bridge at Newstead has also survived and now enjoys listed status, although it is now somewhat dilapidated.

The main shed and overhead crane from Rigley's wagon works found a new home in the 1980s when they were dismantled and moved to the Midland Railway Centre at Butterley. Today the shed houses a collection of preserved coaching stock.

By 1966 the tracks south along the Leen Valley line from Bestwood junction had been lifted. The connection to the GCR remained, but time was running out for the route. The signal protecting the junction has had its arm removed, and the signal box is no longer in use. Bestwood sidings, alongside the Midland route are just visible in the far left of the picture.

Ronald Askew

The GN built this occupational crossing (Bridge No 2) to serve fields east of the line in the area now called Bestwood Park. When the farm land was developed for housing after the war, the bridge became a residential access route, and latterly a pedestrian subway. Known locally as Marble Arch, it was demolished in 1989, partly to remove a maintenance liability, and partly in response to rising social problems in the area.

Bestwood Junction is seen here looking north in 1966, after closure of the route south to Leen Valley Junction and abolition of the signal box. The tracks on this section were lifted too a couple of years later, and the box demolished.

Ronald Askew

O4/2 63644 approaches Bulwell North Junction on the spur from Bestwood.with a loaded coal train in 1962.

Ronald Askew

Unidentified WD Class loco leaving the Leen Valley line at Bulwell North Junction with a Colwick bound coal train in the early 1960s.

Eric Shelton

The Annesley Dido workmans train ran from Bulwell Common to Annesley Shed. It usually comprised antiquated rolling stock withdrawn from front line service, as this photograph demonstrates. The leading coach is a GCR clerestory roofed vehicle, whilst the one behind is vintage GNR flat-roofed stock. This view was recorded at Bulwell in 1958.

Ronald Askew

Signal 19 on the Down Main is set to danger whilst in the background 9F No 92105 draws forward from a rake of empties in the No 2 Colliery reception yard. The station appears to be in remarkably good order, despite being closed for 30 years. After running around and collecting the brake van, the loco will proceed to Butlers Hill, where it will collect a loaded rake for the journey back to Colwick.

Eric Shelton

Class B1 No 61163 is seen on a southbound unfitted working at Hucknall Town in around 1960.

Eric Shelton

An unidentified Austerity is seen in the Down Shunt in Hucknall Town yard in the 1960s. This locomotive was probably one of Colwick's, the shed having a very sizeable allocation of these powerful machines at this time.

Eric Shelton

Ex GNR Class R1 is seen shunting in Hucknall Town yard in the 1920s. 3122 was a Colwick based engine for much of its life and was withdrawn from service in 1933. Note the ash ballast and wide sleeper spacing of the siding in the foreground.

Eric Shelton

The site of Linby Station is seen from the window of a York-Bournemouth Express on the adjacent GCR line in 1966. The GN line had closed by this date and the remaining track was in use for wagon storage.

Ronald Askew

Ex GCR Class B8 is seen passing Linby Colliery in the 1930s with a northbound excursion. The station at Linby was closed by the GNR in 1916 as an economy measure.

Eric Shelton

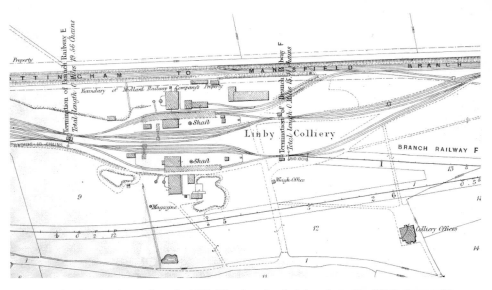

Linby Colliery is shown here in 1880. The drawing is taken from the GNR plan seeking Parliamentary consent for the line. The colliery office seen on the bottom right is visible on the horizon of the photograph opposite.

Author's Collection

Linby Colliery continued to produce coal until 1990 when it closed. A Thomas Hill 0-6-0 Diesel Hydraulic shunter is seen here in the pit yard in April 1988.

Ian Askew

9F No 92096 is seen here at Newstead with a southbound conflat train on 22nd Feb 1965. The signal box was built in LNER days to replace two GNR boxes.

Ronald Askew

Two views of bridge No 24, built to span the approach road to Newstead Abbey taken in December 2005. The quality of detailing and the trouble that the GNR went to in the construction of this bridge can be clearly seen.

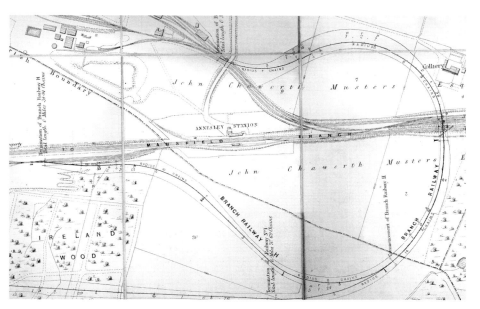

The GNR initially terminated at Annesley Colliery. In 1892 the GCR constructed and end on junction, having tunnelled through Robin Hood's Hill, and in 1899 it became the springboard for the GCRs London Extension.

Author's Collection

The GNR met the GCR at Annesley. Here concentration sidings and a depot sprang up. A GCR Class 8K (O4) is seen coming off Annesley Yard past the GN signal cabin in about 1920.

Ian Trivett Collection

4.3 The Great Central in the Leen Valley

The Manchester, Sheffield and Lincolnshire Railway was a successful company. It owned docks on Humberside and on the Manchester Ship Canal, and it had numerous maritime interests. It served the South Yorkshire and North Nottinghamshire coalfields, transported textiles from Manchester and steel from Sheffield. This comfortable existence was not enough for the Company however. It had aspirations to become more than just a provincial operation. The Chairman of the Board of Directors, Sir Edward Watkin had a grand vision. He wanted an independent fast new link to London, connecting the industrial heartlands of the country with the capital. He succeeded in persuading the Board and 1894 the company gained Parliamentary powers for a new line. A year later construction began of what would be the last main line railway of the classic era.

The choice of starting point for the new line was Annesley, at the head of the Leen Valley. The company had recently completed tunnelling through the Robin Hood Hills, and the Leen Valley ran south towards the first major destination on the new line at Nottingham.

The Company was a relative latecomer, so the route it was forced to occupy needed substantial earthworks and structures to achieve the gentle gradients and generous curves that high speed running demanded. The high construction costs, even with savings generated through use of steam shovels led to the decision to build the route with only two tracks. The cost of earthworks and structures required for additional freight lines were simply prohibitive. The legacy of this decision was that freight trains would need to run at passenger train timings. To aid high speed running, the Company avoided level crossings and the proliferation of local colliery accesses and junctions that characterised other routes in the area.

A concentration facility was provided at Annesley, but other than this, the only colliery link in the area was at Hucknall. Similarly it was sparing in its construction of small wayside stations. The local communities did not fit in with Watkin's strategic vision. They were already served by other companies, and too many local stopping trains would constrain the timetable.

Class 9F No 92011 is seen at Bulwell Common with a northbound mixed freight in around 1962. The simple island platform layout was typical of wayside stations on the London Extension.

Eric Shelton

92075 of Annesley Shed heads south past Bulwell South Junction with a "Windcutter" bound for Woodford Halse. Despite their small driving wheel diameter, 9Fs were known to work these unfitted freights at speeds on occasion exceeding 60mph!

Eric Shelton

Send your interesting old photographs to: The Editor, Hucknall Dispatch, Unit 2A, Sherwood Oaks Business Park, Southwell Road West, Mansfield, Nottinghamshire, NG18 4TB, or e-mail them in jpeg format to newsdesk@hucknall-dispatch.co.uk. Don't forget include your name and postal address, as well as any information you know about the photo.

ese hard-working men are shown building the Manchester, Sheffield and Lincolnshire Railwayat Hucknall Lane, Bulwell Forest, in this early photo-aph, taken in 1897 by S W A Newton of Leicester. The image has been supplied by Nottingham Historical Film Unit.

This week's comments on Twitter and on Facebook

holgatesportsleaders ...
Well done for your hard work and leadership skills! #Holgate #Hucknall @HucknallTourism

@holgatehucknall

Smiles all round for the recent site walk around we arranged for local school children of one of our live @coopuk projects in #Hucknall.

@HBProjects

The excellent @greatfooddrink Big Bake is @Newstead_Abbey in August & we have a handy list of nearby hotels here > http://bit.ly/2sGl5CJ

@VisitNotts

Register for #Clearing and we'll take the stress out of results day by calling you. http://buff.ly/2tom1OV

@DerbyUni

We've had a busy weekend! We danced our socks off at the Brazil Carnival Ball & played football with Robin Hood at Hucknall Sports Fun Day

@NUHCharity

Holgate Sports Leaders

Checkout @LondonFire #TotalRecalls campaign, calling for changes to make all white goods safer http://www.london-fire.gov.uk/total-recalls/what-we-are-calling-for.asp ...

@nottsfire

@DISPATCHDAILY
FACEBOOK: HUCKNALLANDBULWELLDISPATCH
NEWSDESK@HUCKNALL-DISPATCH.CO.UK

Strewn with dog ends

I had a lovely walk into Hucknall today, down High Street. It was a lovely day,, the sun was shining and I was very impressed now it's been pedestrianised.
It was nice to walk and cross over without watching for cars, but I couldn't believe all the cigarette butts all over. Mostly down the right side walking toward the Byron and loads outside the bookies. What a shame.
Probably could do with more bins or the warden could walk down and hand a few fines out.

Miss Davis
By email

PRESERVING FARLEYS SPRING
Leave this landmark be

I now live in Weymouth, Dorset, but occasionally visit family and friends in Hucknall. The last time I was there, at New Year, I was a bit devastated to see so much potentially healthy land unnecessarily disappearing under tarmac/brick/concrete.

This will put an enormous strain on resources and, by its very nature, damage the environment along with having further negative impact o people's health.
I fail to see the "planning" behind such decisions, if we want to see a healthy balance of population and land use. However, I can see at an instance the short-term, profit driven motives for uncaring developers and share-holder and the "kudos" to be gained by health-ignorant councillo to mistakenly think they hav to provide more and more housing for some reason.
If that excuse/reason is popu lation, what are the real facts of the situation, and why is there no real 'planning' for th future?
The logical outcome is there will soon be no land left that not under tarmac/brick/con crete and present inhabitant will just suffer more with po lution and their health, as we as in their pockets.
It's not only Hucknall, but here in Weymouth too, and I suspect many other places.
The words health and planning seem to be a mystery to many, especially with those power to do the right thing. In my opinion it is a poignan reminder of our failing educ tion system.

1981: Demolition of Great Central Viaduct, Hucknall Lane, Bulwell, Nottingham. Picture provided by Reg Baker.

THE VIADUCT ARCHS OVER THE LMS LEEN VALLEY RAILWAY LINE & BESTWOOD ROAD
WERE DEMOLISHED ON THE 1.1.1990 BY A LEEDS DEMOLISHION CONTRACTOR
D. SKILL [20. 2. 2010]

This week's comments on Twitter and on Facebook

We need to thank @LincolnGBrewing for their help

...Cllr Winfield has launched a petition to turn old @NewCollegeNottm #Hucknall building into walk-in centre.
@D2N2EP

I would not eat them even if they gave them away.
Elaine Miller, re 'food of love' oysters reduced to 25p for Valentine's Day

Good result but sadly for the grieving families it won't bring them back, it will just help them find closure.
Debbie Dement, re father and sons found guilty of murdering three people

I stick by what I said Saturday. It's like they had been building 13 matches worth of hate and couldnt wait to boo
@johnnyboy_nottm, re Nottingham Forest fans who booed after Huddersfield Town defeat.

@DISPATCHDAILY
FACEBOOK: HUCKNALLANDBULWELLDISPATCH
NEWSDESK@HUCKNALL-DISPATCH.CO.UK

...board etc would be far more beneficial.
How many residents actually every fortnight could fill to garden waste bins? Answer: not many.
I think the council have missed a better way for the use of the old waste bin.

Adrian Brownlow
By email

PRICING
Help the consumer

The weekly shop is becoming more expensive because of unfair pricing by supermarkets.
The slogan most pronounced by the consumer "you're paying for the branded label" is an economic scandal.
Premium brand items cost more because of manufacturers and retailers charging for the brand name.
This is a well-established fact known to the consumer.
The female consumers who to their credit manage family budgets have been struggling

...ties are funded by donatio... from big business.
The consumer's worries o... the rising cost of living hav... been ignored for too long b... both these political parties... In responding to these concerns about the cost of living, I propose that premium brand pricing ("you're payin... for the branded label") is stopped.
Food bills are being made more expensive by companies and this is reducing the purchasing power of the nation and of the individual.
It is time that consumers benefitted from permanent price reductions.

Oliver Healey
By email

LOCUM SOLUTION
Time to take gloves off

It is time for Junior Doctors to take their gloves off in their fight against the Health Secretary.
Whilst a long term strike might be considered to contravene the Hippocratic Oath,

The line opened to freight in 1899, and passengers the following year. To reflect the newly elevated status of the Company, it changed its name to the Great Central Railway.

Stations in the Leen Valley were provided at Hucknall (Central), Bulwell (Common) and New Basford, with a basic halt at Hollin Well & Annesley. A second halt was later added to serve Bulwell Hall, but not provided with ticket office facilities. Prospective passengers needed to buy their tickets at the clubhouse of the neighbouring golf club! Each station was constructed to a standard layout of one island platform accessed from an overbridge, whilst halts consisted of two simple wooden platforms. Extensive sidings were constructed at Bulwell Common to handle GNR exchange traffic, and junctions at Bulwell connected with that company's Leen Valley and Derbyshire Extension lines.

out Royal Scots discarded by other sheds on the LMR. Annesley Shed was situated in a hard water area, and towards the end of its existence when cleaning was less of a priority, its locos were characterised by white lime scale deposits on the boiler casings and cylinders.

From the 1930s, workmen's trains ran between Bulwell Common and Annesley. These did not appear in the public timetable, and ran along the GNR's Leen Valley line, as a replacement service, following the withdrawal of regular passenger trains on that line. The service became well known in its latter years, and the locomotives selected to work the diagram would often be elderly examples, no longer required for front line service. Through the 1930's an MS&L Sacre 4-4-0 worked the service. Later motive power included Ivatt C12s, Parker F2s and even an ex Great Eastern N7. C12 No 67363 is seen here with some particularly vintage stock on the link between Bulwell North Junction and Bestwood Junction at Bulwell in July 1957.

Ronald Askew

An unidentified class B1 heads south past the junction for the GNR Leen Valley line, with a local passenger service in about 1960. The view was taken from Bulwell North Junction signal box, located just to the north of Bulwell Common station.

Eric Shelton

At Annesley Junction the company built a motive power depot and a marshalling yard. Annesley Shed came to be of strategic importance during the later years of the line, particularly after the closure of Nottingham Shed in 1932. Whilst the Depot was primarily home to freight engines, it had a small allocation of passenger types. In latter years this included Britannia Pacifics and finally worn

Long coal trains would be marshalled at Annesley, their loads originating from several local collieries, via both the GCR and GNR lines. These would then be hauled south to Woodford Halse by the Depots Robinson Q1s, 04s and latterly BR Standard 9F's. Known variously as "Runners" or "Windcutters" these diagrams needed to run very briskly, since the London Extension had few loops, and passenger trains could not be delayed.

An unidentified Austerity heads a southbound coal train off the spur from the GN Leen Valley line towards Bulwell Common at Bulwell North Junction in 1962. Prior to 1960, this working would have been routed to Colwick via the Great Northern Derbyshire extension, through Leen Valley Junction and Mapperley Tunnel.

C A Hill

Bulwell viaduct (Bridge No 289) is seen here from Hucknall Lane, looking north in July 1952. The Home Ales advert on the steel bridge was well known locally and survived until demolition in 1977. The brick arches remained until 1989.

Nottingham City Council

Numerous bridges were required on the Leen Valley portion of the route, the most significant being the 24 span viaduct at Bulwell. Rising to a maximum height of sixty feet, this impressive blue brick faced structure spanned Hucknall Lane, the River Leen, the Midland's Leen Valley line and Bestwood Lane. Hucknall Lane was crossed by a skew steel span, and the course of the River Leen was diverted to accommodate the structure.

In common with the GN Leen Valley line, the GC was transferred to the London Midland in 1958. This was effectively the beginning of the end, and services were gradually run down in favour of duplicate Midland's routes. Leen valley coal was sent to Toton and passengers from Sheffield for London, Leicester or Nottingham travelled by the less direct Midland route (with a reversal at Nottingham after the closure of the Melton line). The line closed as a through route in 1967. The site of Annesley yards and shed were quickly buried under colliery spoil from nearby pits.

Station sites have all been reclaimed and the mighty viaduct at Bulwell is no more, the final portion having been demolished by Nottingham City Council in 1989. Today the sole remains of the Great Central's London Extension are a few gaunt sections of severed embankment near Hucknall.

Hucknall Central was the next station north from Bulwell Common (excluding Bulwell Hall Halt). The platform buildings were to the standard GCR design and they are seen here in 1964.

Ronald Askew

The platform arrangements at Hucknall were typical for the GCR, but a larger Booking Office was provided at road level, with a footbridge connecting to the platform. A southbound coal train is seen here passing through the station in the charge of 9F 92031 on 2nd March 1963.

Ronald Askew

Annesley Yards were controlled by a series of large signal cabins, of which the No 4 box is seen here. The view was recorded in 1924, whilst the box still wore the green livery of the Great Central Railway.

Ian Trivett Collection

A Marylebone express hurries past Annesley Yard in March 1924. The train is in the charge of "Lord Faringdon" Class No 5428 (LNER B7). The details of the photographer are not known.

Ian Trivett Collection

A group of enginemen and shunters pose for the camera in front of an unidentified Parker Class N5 at Annesley Yard in about 1924.

Ian Trivett Collection

Annesley South Junction signal box was unusual in that it was partly stone-built. The majority of signal cabins on the London Extension were either entirely timber, or built with brick bases. The LNER was a new company when this photograph was taken in 1924, and the signalling was still pure GCR.

Ian Trivett Collection

Annesley Shed was situated at some distance from any major population centre. Many of the shed and yard personnel would have used the Annesley Dido daily workman's train to get to work. This commuted between Bulwell Common (where it is photographed) and the halt at Annesley South Junction. July 1957.

Ronald Askew

This view of Annesley shed taken 28th July 1964 shows Rebuilt Royal Scot No 46125 resting between duties. Class 8F and 9F freight locomotives can also be seen in the background.

Ronald Askew

A distant view of Annesley shed reveals a line up of freight engine classes awaiting their turn of duty. Today this site is buried beneath a mountain of colliery waste. 28th July 1964.

Ronald Askew

Four views taken by the late Eric Shelton in the early 60s portray the dirty conditions that prevailed at Annesley, especially towards the end of its life. The colliery's aerial ropeway can be seen behind the shed and the filthy condition of many of the engines has rendered them unidentifiable.

Top left and right photographs show grimy class 9Fs on shed awaiting turns of duty.

Bottom left shows a surprisingly clean Stanier 8F 48282, with an unidentified Austerity behind it

Bottom right shows 9F No 92011 out of use and backed on to an old Barnum coach in use as a mess to the side of the shed.

4.4 The Robin Hood Line

Early in the 1980s a consortium of District and County Councils was formed to investigate reopening the former Midland line through to Mansfield. Funding was to be procured from a variety of sources including the partner Authorities, the EEC, and BR. The two County Councils (Notts and Derbys), together with BR would lead the investigation / feasibility work with a view to having the line reopened to Worksop by 1992. The timescale and economics would prove to be unrealistic so a phased reopening was planned instead.

BR obtained Parliamentary powers in mid-1990, and the project moved into the construction phase. Section One saw the section from Mansfield junction to Newstead upgraded and resignalled. Much of the old mechanical signalling went, and new stations were built on the former locations of Bulwell Market and Hucknall Byron, with a further station and temporary terminus just south of the old Newstead station site. The first passenger trains ran in 1993.

Section Two of the project was more ambitious, requiring total reconstruction of a little over two miles of lost railway, allowing trains to reach Mansfield again. Immediately north of Newstead, land to each side of the original embankment had been filled with colliery spoil.

Contractor's tracklaying equipment is seen near the site of the old station at Annesley in June 1996. Since no existing tracks were in place, temporary rails had to be run out in order to place new track panels.

Deep beneath this an underground fire smouldered away and wisps of sulphurous smoke emerged from fissures close to the alignment, giving rise to concerns about ground stability. The ground levels monitored for movement as construction proceeded. Fortunately none was detected.

The curving embankment that approached Kirkby tunnel had been removed some years earlier, so this had to be replaced. Likewise the buried tunnel had to be re-excavated and many tonnes of shale removed.

The northern portal of Kirkby Tunnel is seen in June 1996. The arch facings were rebuilt after they partially collapsed, shortly after the structure was re-excavated. Rails were laid a week after this photograph was taken.

County Council Engineers employed old ordnance survey maps, together with the Author's archive of old photographs to give an approximate location of the southern portal. In early 1988 a trial excavation was made and fortunately it landed on the crown of the arch face at the first attempt, some twenty feet down. The fill inside the tunnel had settled, allowing a preliminary inspection of the arch, but a full inspection was only possible after the fill had been removed.

There had been concern about subsidence, since coal had been extracted beneath the line after it had closed. These fears were unfounded however, with the tunnel proving to be in reasonably sound condition. The lining had been badly scored by the blades of bulldozers pushing spoil into the bore, but this spoil may have helped the bore resist stresses induced by ground movement. The heavy masonry parapets had been pushed off, but these were recovered, repaired and put back. The damaged bore was repointed (BR rejected a proposal to apply a 100mm thick "Gunnite" spray concrete lining,), but HMRI concern about clearances led to the track being relayed through the tunnel as a single line.

The B6201 overbridge to the north of Kirkby Tunnel had been underfilled, and once re-excavated it was found that a new deck was needed. A residential development had also encroached onto the filled cutting between the bridge and the tunnel, so this was purchased and demolished. The route north of here was lost beneath development, so the alignment was slewed to pick up a short section of the abandoned GNR route.

The GN line had been situated in a cutting, and part of this had been filled with domestic refuse some years previously. The new line needed to be at a higher level, and Notts County Council Engineers took the decision to leave the waste undisturbed. The fill was compacted and capped with a clay blanket, and a complex methane gas venting system was installed. Levels were then raised to formation with colliery shale.

Ballast is graded to level on the section of alignment that follows the line of the old GNR. The rock formation in the background is the extreme top of the original cutting. The earthworks on the project were designed by Notts County Council, and British Rail designed the structures, signalling and permanent way.

At Kirkby the new line connected with the line from Pye Bridge. This was upgraded and resignalled, and new stations were built at Kirkby and Mansfield. The original Mansfield Town station building had been sold out of railway use, and the old train shed demolished. The goods shed remained standing however, and this was modified to create an attractive new train shed for the reborn station.

Train services to Mansfield began in November 1996, but were suspended shortly after when a section of continuously welded rail snapped. It transpired that the rail tension was incorrect so all new rails had to be checked and adjusted, before services resumed.

Section three allowed passenger services to resume all the way to Worksop and Shirebrook over more freight only line, completing the project. At the time of writing, a little over a decade after completion, passenger figures are healthy, and the scheme has proven to be a real success story.

A Nottingham bound Class 156 Departs Newstead Station in wintry conditions on 27/12/05. The new station is approximately on the site of the original, opposite the appropriately named Station Hotel.

This was not quite the final chapter in the story however. The section of line between Basford and Hucknall was substantially revised in 2001/2, with new signals and removal of the remaining signal boxes at Lincoln Street and Bestwood Park. Bulwell Station was reduced to one platform and the route from Bulwell to Hucknall was made single line. This work was to create room for construction of the northern section of the NET tram line to its Hucknall terminus.

5. The Ambergate, Nottingham, Boston & Eastern Junction Railway

The line connecting Nottingham with Grantham was built by a small independent company named the Ambergate, Nottingham, Boston & East Junction Railway, and opened in 1850. This ambitiously named company never actually reached any of the destinations in its title, but did succeed in constructing 22 miles of line from Grantham to Colwick. A junction here with the Midland Railway's line between Nottingham and Lincoln allowed the Ambergate to run trains on Midland metals into Nottingham itself.

In 1852 the Great Northern "Towns Line" arrived at Grantham and a connection was built to the eastern end of the Ambergate's line. Operation of GNR services over the route into Nottingham led to disagreement with the Midland Railway (see Volume 1) and difficulty of access to its metals. The ANB&EJR amalgamated with the GN in 1855, and operated as part of that company's larger network, with trains running in to the new GNR terminus at London Road from 1857.

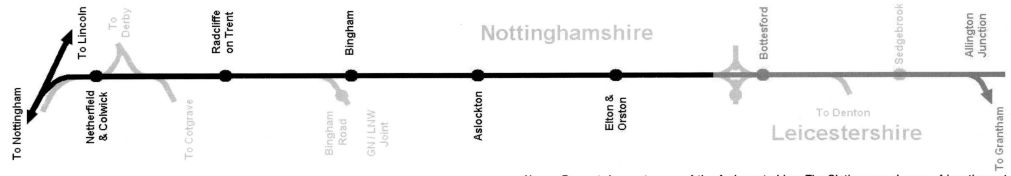

Above: Present day route map of the Ambergate Line. The Sixties saw closure of junctions at Bottesford and Saxondale, and colliery / quarry branches closed in the decades that followed. Branches marked in pale grey are no longer in existence.

Left: Grantham marked the eastern end of the Ambergate line. From 1852 trains for Colwick ran from the GNR station on the new East Coast Main Line, the original Ambergate terminus being downgraded to goods only. A century later in February 1955, D R Morley made the journey, with his camera. B1 No 61248 is seen at the south end of Grantham with a local train from Lincoln. Nottingham trains at this time would have comprised similar stock.

N(B)MRS / D R Morley

The stations on the line were built along similar lines, and generally comprised two facing platforms, although in the case of Sedgebrook and Bottesford they were staggered. Substantial brick built two storey buildings housed the Stationmasters accommodation, with single storey booking hall, parcels office, waiting rooms and toilets attached. Attention to detail included stone mullioned windows and ornate chimney stacks, resulting in a generally pleasing appearance. Crossing Keepers cottages and associated structures on the line were built to a similar architectural style, with steeply pitched roofs and high gables.

Station facilities were modified and developed under GNR operation, and in the case of Bingham and Radcliffe on Trent, wrought iron footbridges were erected. With the introduction of block signalling in 1870, the company also constructed many of its ornate and characteristic signal boxes, and subsequently equipped the line with its distinctive somersault signals.

Colwick B1 No 61376 is seen with the 16.05 Nottm – Grantham at Aslockton on 28th Feb 1955. It was photographed from the 16.08 train, ex- Grantham, with the photographer travelling to Netherfield and Colwick.

N(B)MRS / D R Morley

Netherfield & Colwick station is seen here in the snow at around 16.50. The 16.08 Grantham train has left and dusk is closing in. This most westerly of the stations on the original line was reconstructed ten years after this view was taken.

N(B)MRS / D R Morley

1875 saw the completion of the GNR / LNWR branch, running from Saxondale Junction near Bingham to Marefield Junction by way of Melton Mowbray. London & North Western Railway services from Northampton accessed the joint line here, running through to Nottingham London Road by agreement, whilst GNR services from the newly built Leicester Belgrave Road Station used the line to connect the two cities. The joint line formed part of a web of secondary routes in the area, and a connection from the joint line at Stathern to Newark in the north crossed under the Grantham line at Bottesford, with chords connecting in each direction. Numerous ironstone quarries took access from these lines, and by the late nineteenth century the picturesque Vale of Belvoir was criss-crossed with branches. Station buildings on the Joint were generally modest hipped-roof single storey brick structures, owing much in appearance to LNWR influence, whilst signal boxes and associated signals were to GNR designs.

The Ambergate line was upgraded in the 1870's to include separate goods lines between Saxondale Junction and Radcliffe on Trent. This was to accommodate the additional traffic, and particularly ironstone trains associated with the Joint line and the branch to Denton.

Traffic was plentiful on the line during the late Nineteenth Century, with the GNR's largest distribution yard at Colwick in the west, and a direct link to London in the east. Even after the arrival of the GCR's London Extension in 1900 the line continued to be busy, with GN passenger services now routed into Nottingham Victoria in place of London Road.

During the First World War a GNR train travelling from Grantham to Nottingham inadvertently became the cause of Nottingham being bombed. On the night of 23rd September, of a flight of seven Zeppelins set out on a bombing mission from Germany, with Nottingham their target. Navigation at night has been a problem since aviation began and in 1916 navigators had few aids to help them. Of the seven airships, only one found itself in remotely the right area. L17 was blindly groping for its target in the northern reaches of the Vale of Belvoir when its crew spotted the lights of a westbound passenger train. Blackout precautions were scant during the First World War, and following the train led the Zeppelin to the city. Consequently Nottingham was subjected to the first aerial attack in its history.

Sadly it would not be the last, as would prove to be the case 25 years later.

Bottesford West Junction provided connections with the branch to Newark to the north and with the LNW joint line to the south. The south link was abandoned in 1966, and the north in 1982. The signal box remained in use as a block post and is seen here in June 2005.

The Grantham Line and the Joint line both suffered damage during the Second World War. In May 1941 German bombs fell at Bottesford and further south around Stathern. These rural lines are unlikely to have been singled out for attack, and it is more probable that decoy lights in the Vale of Belvoir lured bombers away from their objective of Nottingham.

In 1952 a branch opened to the east of Rectory Junction to serve the new colliery at Cotgrave, generating further traffic. This was to represent the final development of the route however. From 1958 changing BR regional management and shifting economics were to cause more damage to the GN network than Hitler's bombs had managed to achieve. A downturn in traffic led to the run down and ultimate closure of Colwick Yard in favour of Toton. Cheap foreign iron ore saw an end to ironstone quarrying in the area and falling passenger receipts had already led to the closure of Sedgebrook Station in 1956. The joint line closed in 1962, and the network of connecting lines and industrial branches followed shortly after. Even the Cotgrave branch would be relatively short lived, closing in 1988.

In 1964 the connection to the Midland at Netherfield was reinstated, and with the run down of the GCR and closure of Nottingham Victoria, Grantham services were diverted into Nottingham Midland.

Nottingham-Grantham Diesel Train

A new lightweight diesel train which has been put into service to-day between Nottingham and Grantham. the train seats 127 passengers and weighs 47¼ tons.

Diesel railcars were introduced on the Nottingham – Grantham service in the late Fifties as part of BR's modernisation plan. The new units were cleaner and cheaper to operate than their steam counterparts, and gave the passenger a much clearer vantage point than in the old Gresley suburban stock.

Nottm Evening Post

After closure of the LNW Joint lines in 1962, the goods lines west of Saxondale junction were taken out. The remaining lines were slued across, and for the next few years some innovative permanent way activities took place on the vacant trackbed. The Government of the day was underwriting construction of a rail tunnel to France, and the construction form of the tunnel precluded the use of traditional ballasted track. BR's researchers were tasked with developing a trackform with a continuous concrete bed. The test site chosen was at Radcliffe on Trent, and in the early Seventies a number of different systems were built and tested. The tunnel project was abandoned in 1975, but BR engineers gained a valuable insight into construction techniques that would be developed on later projects, including the Channel Tunnel Rail Link, and more locally, the Nottingham Express Transit (NET) scheme.

THIS SUPERSEDES HANDBILL
PP/244/30

BRITISH RAILWAYS

SPECIAL CHEAP DAY TICKETS

ANY DAY   ANY TRAIN

NOTTINGHAM

(VICTORIA AND LONDON ROAD)

GRANTHAM

AND   INTERMEDIATELY

AVAILABLE OUTWARD AND RETURN ON DAY OF ISSUE IN EITHER DIRECTION BETWEEN THE FOLLOWING STATIONS AT THE THIRD CLASS FARES SHOWN

Nottingham (Victoria and London Road)								
s. d.								
8	Netherfield & Colwick							
	s. d.							
1 4	9	Radcliffe-on-Trent						
		s. d.						
1 9	1 1	8	Bingham					
			s. d.					
1 11	1 8	1 4	8	Aslockton				
				s. d.				
2 0	1 11	1 6	10	5	Elton & Orston			
					s. d.			
2 5	2 3	1 8	1 4	8	5	Bottesford		
						s. d.		
2 9	2 5	2 2	1 10	1 6	1 4	8	Sedgebrook	
							s. d.	
3 4	2 11	2 9	2 5	1 11	1 9	1 8	10	Grantham

First class special cheap day tickets are also issued at approximately 50 per cent. over the third class fares

SEE OVER FOR DETAILS OF TRAIN SERVICE

Further information will be supplied on application to stations, offices, agencies or to W. B. Carter, District Commercial Superintendent, Derby (Tel : Derby 42442) ; A. G. Croxall, District Commercial Superintendent, Peterborough (Tel : Peterborough 4221); or C. Dandridge, Commercial Superintendent, Liverpool Street station, London, E.C.2 (Tel : BIShopsgate 7600)

CONDITIONS OF ISSUE

These tickets are issued subject to the British Transport Commission's published Regulations and Conditions applicable to British Railways exhibited at their stations or obtainable free of charge at station booking offices

LUGGAGE ALLOWANCES are as set out in these general notices

Children under three years of age, free ; three years and under fourteen, half-fares

London, September 1954

Published by British Railways (Eastern Region)   Printed in Great Britain   Stafford & Co., Ltd., Netherfield, Nottingham
PP/244/60

The GN/LNW Joint line closed in 1962. It is seen here two decades later, roughly halfway between Bingham Road and Barnstone Stations. The formation was still in good condition, and an LNER concrete PW hut remained in place.

Gradual modernisation and maintenance renewals have seen progressive removal of pre-nationalisation semaphore signalling and mechanical signal boxes on the route. The abandonment of the joint lines in 1962 led to removal of boxes at Saxondale and Bottesford, whilst rationalisation and reduction of stations to unstaffed halts in 1968 saw wholesale loss of station buildings and signal boxes. Nearer to Grantham, Allington Junction box was demolished in October 2005. An interesting feature in this box was the original gradient diagram, which right up to the abolition of the box showed details of the line right through to the long closed Nottingham Victoria.

Today GNR boxes survive at Bottesford West, Bingham and Rectory Junction, albeit with new windows, refurbished interiors and modern BR block equipment (although original GNR block bells were still in use at the former two in 2005). Rectory Junction box is scheduled for abolition by 2010, and once it has gone, no mechanical boxes will remain in the immediate vicinity of the Nottingham conurbation. No GNR or LNER semaphore signals now remain on the Grantham line, the last ones at Bottesford West being removed in 2003. Pockets of BR upper quadrant types on steel posts remain however, and seem likely to continue in use for some time to come.

After years of relative neglect, the line benefited from major investment in 2005 with the opening of a new chord connecting with the East Coast Main Line north of Grantham This allows greater flexibility of train operation and can only increase traffic on the route, which should help to assure its long term future.

A long term aspiration held by local Authorities for the line is the re-opening of the Cotgrave Colliery Branch. Proposals include a park and ride site by the A52 with shuttle services into Nottingham. More ambitiously an extension is proposed through to join the severed Midland line to Melton Mowbray and on to Kettering, to permit reopening of passenger services. Both schemes would require substantial sums of money, and given present Government attitudes towards public transport funding their chances of success are slim.

In the early Eighties one route development to meet with more success was conversion of two miles of the abandoned Joint line south from the site of Bingham Road station. Public access was constructed, a crushed stone pathway laid, and trees planted to create a linear woodland walk. This was crossed by the line of the A52 Bingham Bypass in 1986. Where the new bypass crossed the route a prefabricated culvert was placed over the track bed and the surrounding cutting filled to permit construction of the road. Interestingly during construction, Contractors came across the fallen remains of a semaphore signal.

The walk terminates a little south of the A52, and from here, the trackbed has either been left to nature or ploughed over by local farmers.

A westbound Central Trains Class 170 multiple unit pulls forward to signal NJ31 to await right of way on 06/06/05. The central platform bay accommodated a headshunt until 1960 .

Netherfield & Colwick was built by the GNR in 1878, at the junction for the GNR's Derbyshire Extension of 1875. The through route closed in 1960 but a spur remained open to Gedling Colliery. A pair of Toton based Class 20s are seen here coming off the branch in 1983.

Netherfield Junction box was commissioned after Netherfield & Colwick station was rebuilt in 1960, It replaced an earlier cabin that had been built into the station buildings. When the connection to the Midland was reinstated in 1964 the box became considerably busier.

The original 79 lever Railway Signalling Company frame in Rectory Junction box has been shortened considerably, but many of the remaining levers have since become redundant, as the white paint shows. In its heyday this box controlled the eastern entry to Colwick Yards. It would have been continuously manned with several personnel needed to work it, including telegraph lads to make entries in the Train Register.

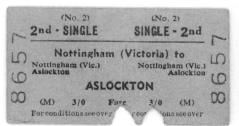 

Examples of tickets for journeys on the line dating from the 1960s. By the time these were issued, passenger services were dieselised and the writing was on the wall for Nottingham Victoria.

Author's Collection

Rectory Junction box is the last survivor of four large cabins that controlled the complex of lines at Colwick. Situated at the eastern outlet of the yard, it also controlled the Derbyshire Extension's eastern leg that skirted around the yards.

A Central Trains Class 158 approaches Rectory Junction box with a Nottingham train on 06/06/05, The trailing junction to the left serves an oil terminal.

The line has seen numerous special workings, and in early 1984 A3 pacific 4472 Flying Scotsman is seen crossing the Trent with the westbound leg of The Fensman.

Radcliffe on Trent station was reduced to unstaffed status in 1968. Most of the original buildings were demolished, and bus shelters erected in place. By 1982 only one of the original buildings on the Down platform survived. Today even this has gone and residential development now encroaches right to the up platform.

Passenger services from the early sixties were almost exclusively worked by Cravens, Swindon and 107 units. A Cravens unit is seen crossing the River Trent with a Grantham to Nottingham train in February 1983.

An ex GNR Class J6 is seen to the east of Radcliffe on Trent, working a loaded ironstone train. This rare, if rather poor photo dates from 1923. Sadly the photographers details are unknown.

Ian Trivett Collection

GNR Class J6 & J4 freight locos are seen near Radcliffe on Trent working light towards Colwick in about 1923. The goods lines were constructed when the GN / LNW Joint line opened, and removed in 1962.

Ian Trivett Collection

Bingham signal cabin is the survivor of a pair that once controlled the station. Seen in June 2005, it is in a good state of repair with decorative bargeboards and GN nameboards still in place. It is possible to see from the brickwork where the box has been extended.

Bingham Station is seen here in 1984. The single storey booking hall and waiting room on the main platform were demolished when the station became unstaffed in 1968. A decade on from this photograph the GNR footbridge would be replaced with a modern steel example.

The frame in Bingham Signal Box was made by the Railway Signal Company and dates from around 1890. The instruments are more recent replacements, being the Standard BR bakelite cased variety.

The GNR design wrought iron footbridge (28A) at Bingham Station is seen here in 1984.

Bingham Station frontage in early 1984. Much of the single storey portion of the building has been demolished, and a second storey extension added.

GREAT NORTHERN RAILWAY
PUBLIC WARNING NOT TO TRESPASS

PERSONS TRESPASSING UPON ANY RAILWAYS BELONGING OR LEASED TO OR WORKED BY THE GREAT NORTHERN RAILWAY COMPANY SOLELY OR IN CONJUNCTION WITH ANY OTHER COMPANY OR COMPANIES, ARE LIABLE TO A PENALTY OF FORTY SHILLINGS UNDER THE GREAT NORTHERN RAILWAY ACT 1896, AND IN ACCORDANCE WITH THE PROVISIONS OF THE SAID ACT PUBLIC WARNING IS HEREBY GIVEN TO ALL PERSONS NOT TO TRESPASS UPON THE SAID RAILWAYS.

KING'S CROSS. JULY 1896.   BY ORDER.

GNR
BEWARE OF TRAINS.

In the early Eighties there were still reminders of the old GNR to be found at Bingham. These cast iron notices were removed in the late Eighties, no doubt to adorn some collector's wall.

Aslockton Station suffered less at the hands of demolition crews than other stations on the line, and retained much of its steam era atmosphere. A Cravens Unit working from Skegness is seen here in 1984. The goods yard to the left has since been replaced with housing.

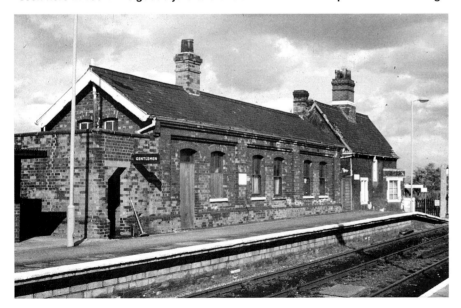

The original Ambergate company buildings survive at Aslockton The Station House differed from others in facing at right angles to the railway. Blue and white enamel signs still adorned the station when photographed in 1984.

The wooden crossing gates at Aslockton remained in use into the 1990s, and in 1984 they still carried LNER oil lamps.

A tidy ANB&EJR timber waiting room on the down platform completed the scene at Aslockton Station in 1984. This is the last survivor of this design of building, and sadly it is just a gutted shell at the time of writing.

Bottesford Station was similar architecturally to Bingham, and in common with that station, was ruthlessly butchered in 1968. By 1984 only the Stationmasters house remained, together with the railway cottages and crossing keepers house seen in the distance.

Less survives at Elton & Orston Station than others on the line, including even Sedgebrook which closed in 1962. No buildings remain and in this 1984 view, apart from the platforms the only connections with earlier days are decaying ganger's trolley and a timber gate.

A Class 107 DMU arrives at Bottesford Station with a Nottingham train. A goods yard and warehouse once existed to the right of the tracks. By 1984 it was wasteland and today, like Aslockton it is occupied by a housing estate.

The GNR Type 1 signal cabin at Allington Junction marked the divergence of the Sleaford line. The box was passed over for major refurbishment because of its planned replacement. Consequently it retained many of its pre-group features right to the end. It is seen here in 1999.

Time ran out for Allington Junction box on 2nd October 2005. It was rapidly reduced to rubble and dispatched to a recycling plant at Widnes. The newly commissioned panel box is seen in the background.

Allington Junction box was built in 1870 and survived until 2005 when a replacement cabin was commissioned as part of the new chord connecting with the East Coast Main Line. It is seen here, stripped out immediately prior to demolition.

The last LNER signal installation to be removed from the Grantham line was the bracket Up Home signal at Bottesford West Junction. It is seen here in August 2003, by which time it had clearly developed foundation problems.

TRAIN SERVICE BETWEEN NOTTINGHAM AND GRANTHAM

20th SEPTEMBER 1954 until further notice

WEEKDAYS

			a.m.	a.m.	a.m.	a.m.	a.m.	a.m.	a.m.	a.m.	p.m.	p.m.	SO p.m.	ThSX p.m.	ThO p.m.	SO p.m.	SO p.m.	SO p.m.	SX p.m.	SO p.m.	p.m.	p.m.
NOTTINGHAM	Victoria	dep.	5 25	7 0	7 33	7 56	8 25	9 41	10 40	11 33	12 5	12 42	12 55	12 55	12 55	1 20	1 45	1 45	2 18	4 5	4 35
	London Rd. High Level	arr.	5 27	7 2	7 35	7 58	8 27	9 43	10 42	11 35	12 7	12 44	12 57	12 57	12 57	1 22	1 47	1 47	2 20	4 7	4 37
		dep.	5 28	7 4	7 37	7 59	8 28	9 46	10 44	11 37	12 8	12 45	12 58	12 58	12 58	1 23	1 48	1 49	2 21	4 9	4 39
Netherfield and Colwick		,,	5 34	7 10	7 43	8 5	8 37	9 52	10 50	11 43	12 14	12 51	1 4	1 4	1 4	1 29	1 54	1 55	2 27	4 15	4 45
Radcliffe-on-Trent		,,	5 41	7 16	7 49	—	8 43	9 58	10 56	11 49	12 19	..	1 10	1 10	1 10	..	2 0	2 1	2 33	4 22	4 51
Bingham		,,	5 49	7 23	7 56	..	8 51	10 5	11 4	11 56	..	..	1 17	1 17	1 17	..	2 7	2 8	2 40	4 29	4 57
Aslockton		,,	5 53	7 27	..	..	8 55	10 9	11 8	..	..	..	..	1 21	1 21	..	2 11	2 12	2 44	4 34	..
Elton and Orston		,,	5 57	7 31	..	..	8 59	10 13	11 12	..	..	..	..	1 25	1 25	..	..	2 16	2 48	4 38	..
Bottesford		,,	6 4	7 37	8 6	..	9 5	10 19	11 19	..	..	..	..	1 31	1 31	..	2 20	2 23	2 55	4 44	..
Sedgebrook		,,	..	7 43	..	..	9 11	10 25	11 25	..	..	..	..	..	1 39	..	..	2 28	3 1	4 50	..
GRANTHAM		arr.	6 16	7 52	8 18	..	9 19	10 35	11 34	12 18	..	..	..	..	1 48	..	2 34	2 36	3 10	4 59	..

WEEKDAYS—continued / SUNDAYS

			p.m.	p.m.	p.m.	p.m.	p.m.	p.m.	p.m.	p.m.	p.m.	p.m.	SX p.m.	SO p.m.	a.m.	a.m.	p.m.	p.m.	p.m.	p.m.
NOTTINGHAM	Victoria	dep.	5 6	5 16	5 35	6 5	6 10	6 32	7 10	8 3	9 16	10 6	11 0	11 0	9 5	11 0	1 10	5 15	8 15	10 55
	London Rd. High Level	arr.	5 8	5 18	5 37	6 7	6 12	6 34	7 12	8 5	9 18	10 8	..	..	..	..	..	..	..	..
		dep.	5 10	5 19	5 38	6 8	6 14	6 35	7 13	8 7	9 19	10 9	..	..	..	..	..	..	..	..
Netherfield & Colwick		,,	5 16	5 25	5 44	6 14	6 20	6 41	7 19	8 13	9 26	10 15	11 7	11 7	9 12	11 7	1 17	5 22	8 22	..
Radcliffe-on-Trent		,,	5 22	—	5 50	..	6 26	..	7 26	8 19	9 32	10 21	11 13	11 13	9 18	11 13	1 23	5 28	8 28	..
Bingham		,,	5 29	..	5 57	..	6 33	..	7 33	8 27	9 39	10 28	11 21	11 21	9 25	11 20	1 30	5 35	8 35	11 12
Aslockton		,,	5 34	..	6 1	..	6 37	..	..	8 31	9 43	10 32	11 27	11 27	9 29	11 24	1 34	5 39	8 39	11 18
Elton and Orston		,,	5 38	..	6 5	..	6 41	..	..	8 35	9 47	10 36	..	11 31	9 33	..	..	5 43	..	..
Bottesford		,,	5 44	..	..	..	6 47	..	..	8 41	9 53	10 42	11 36	11 36	9 39	11 32	1 42	5 49	8 47	11 27
Sedgebrook		,,	5 49	..	..	..	6 53	..	..	8 47	..	..	..	..	..	..	..	..	..	..
GRANTHAM		arr.	5 57	..	..	..	7 2	..	..	8 56	10 7	10 55	11 49	11 49	9 53	11 47	1 57	6 4	9 0	11 39

WEEKDAYS

			a.m.	a.m.	a.m.	a.m.	a.m.	a.m.	a.m.	a.m.	a.m.	a.m.	SO p.m.	SO p.m.	p.m.	p.m.	ThSX p.m.	ThO p.m.	SO p.m.	p.m.	p.m.
GRANTHAM		dep.	4 55	..	6 36	..	..	7 48	..	8 58	9 40	11 2	..	12 28	12 57	..	..	1 31	3 0	3 20	
Sedgebrook		,,	..	..	..	..	..	7 56	..	9 6	9 48	11 10	..	..	1 5	..	..	1 39	3 8	..	
Bottesford		,,	5 6	..	6 47	..	..	8 2	..	9 12	9 54	11 16	..	12 39	1 11	..	1 45	1 45	3 14	..	
Elton and Orston		,,	..	..	6 52	..	..	8 7	..	9 17	9 59	11 21	..	..	1 16	..	1 50	1 50	3 19	..	
Aslockton		,,	5 13	..	6 56	..	..	8 11	..	9 21	10 3	11 25	..	..	1 20	..	1 54	1 54	3 23	..	
Bingham		,,	5 18	..	6 59	7 44	..	8 16	..	9 26	10 8	11 30	..	..	1 25	..	1 59	1 59	3 28	3 39	
Radcliffe-on-Trent		,,	5 25	..	7 8	7 51	..	8 23	..	9 33	10 15	11 37	12 31	..	1 32	..	2 6	2 6	3 35	3 46	
Netherfield and Colwick		,,	5 32	5 53	7 15	7 57	8 17	8 29	8 47	9 39	10 21	11 46	12 37	..	1 38	1 51	2 12	2 12	3 41	3 52	
NOTTINGHAM	London Rd. High Level	arr.	5 44	5 59	7 21	8 3	8 23	8 35	8 53	9 45	10 27	11 52	12 43	1 1	1 44	1 57	2 18	2 18	3 47	3 58	
		dep.	5 46	6 0	7 24	8 4	8 24	8 36	8 54	9 46	10 29	11 54	12 45	1 3	1 45	1 58	2 19	2 19	3 52	3 59	
	Victoria	arr.	5 48	6 2	7 26	8 6	8 26	8 38	8 56	9 48	10 31	11 56	12 49	1 5	1 47	2 0	2 21	2 21	3 54	4 1	

WEEKDAYS—continued / SUNDAYS

			SX p.m.	p.m.	p.m.	p.m.	p.m.	p.m.	p.m.	p.m.	p.m.	p.m.	a.m.	a.m.	p.m.	p.m.	p.m.
GRANTHAM		dep.	..	4 8	..	5 30	..	6 10	..	8 47	10 0	11 15	7 40	11 0	1 15	6 30	8 35
Sedgebrook		,,	..	4 16	..	5 38	..	6 18	..	8 55	..	..	..	..	..	..	..
Bottesford		,,	..	4 22	..	5 44	..	6 24	..	9 1	10 12	11 27	7 51	11 11	1 26	6 41	8 46
Elton and Orston		,,	..	4 27	..	5 49	..	6 29	7 59	9 6	10 17	..	7 56	..	..	6 46	..
Aslockton		,,	..	4 31	..	5 53	..	6 33	8 3	9 10	10 21	11 34	8 0	11 18	1 33	6 50	8 53
Bingham		,,	..	4 36	5 18	5 58	..	6 38	8 8	9 15	10 26	11 39	8 5	11 23	1 38	6 55	8 58
Radcliffe-on-Trent		,,	..	4 43	5 25	6 5	..	6 45	8 15	9 22	10 33	11 46	8 12	11 30	1 45	7 2	9 5
Netherfield and Colwick		,,	4 37	4 49	5 31	6 11	6 18	6 52	8 21	9 28	10 40	11 54	8 18	11 36	1 51	7 8	9 11
NOTTINGHAM	London Rd. High Level	arr.	4 43	4 55	5 37	6 17	6 24	6 58	8 27	9 34	10 46	..	..	..	..	..	..
		dep.	4 45	4 58	5 39	6 20	6 26	7 0	8 28	9 37	10 49	..	..	..	..	..	..
	Victoria	arr.	4 47	5 0	5 41	6 22	6 28	7 2	8 30	9 39	10 51	12 2	8 29	11 43	2 2	7 15	9 18

SO—Saturdays only   SX—Saturdays excepted   ThO—Thursdays only   ThSX—Thursdays and Saturdays excepted

6. By Midland to Melton

During the 1870's it became apparent to the Midland Railway, that they needed a more direct link from Nottingham to London. The service offered by the GNR from London Road via Grantham was proving more attractive to passengers destined for the Capital and the Midland was losing patronage.

A Class 3 tank hauls empty stock past London Road Junction in about 1960. The box controlled the junction for the Melton line, and entry to the carriage sidings. The box was demolished in 1969 when the junction was lifted. The train shed of the original GNR station at London Road can be seen in the background.

Eric Shelton

The Company was compelled to do something, and the solution lay in a new line from a junction to the east of the Midland's existing Station on Station Street, to Melton Mowbray. The line met the Leicester, Kettering, St Pancras route here and this allowed trains from Sheffield, Leeds and the north to run through Nottingham and on to London, without needing to reverse back out to Trent Junction.

Construction of the line to Melton Mowbray began in 1887, and it opened in November 1879. London trains were diverted to the new route early the following year, and the line was an immediate commercial success, with the direct service to London and improved timetable and shorter journey times winning back much of the patronage lost to the GNR over the preceding decade.

With the new route to London being the most direct, the Midland Railway reclassified its existing mileages, and new mileposts were installed on all routes radiating from Nottingham, with the distance measured via the Melton line.

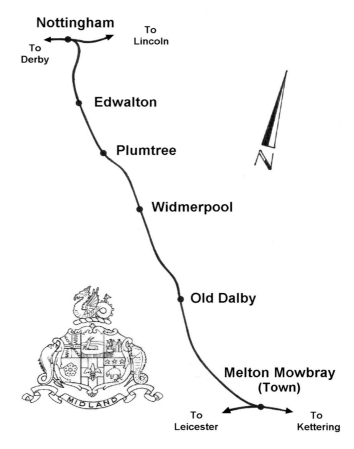

The line turned south from London Road Junction, before crossing the River Trent . By the time it was opened in 1879, suburbs were starting to spring up south of the river. From Edwalton south, the line traversed a rural landscape devoid of industry or any substantial settlement.

There were four intermediate stations on the line, at Edwalton, Plumtree, Widmerpool and Old Dalby. The communities they served were small, and the stations were situated a little way from them. Despite this the facilities were surprisingly generous. Each station was constructed with facing platforms, and substantial blocks of buildings that incorporated the Stationmasters accommodation on one platform, whilst single storey brick built waiting rooms were provided on the other.

The station buildings were constructed using local red brick, relieved with contrasting yellow brick strings, and detailed in an Italianate style similar to that adopted by the Great Northern. The goods yards were provided with well built single road brick sheds with sufficient space for three vehicles to be unloaded inside. Yard facilities also included end on loading ramps permitting wheeled vehicles to be driven onto flat bed wagons.

The line traversed an increasingly undulating landscape as it headed south. Much of it had to be constructed on cutting or embankment. The most substantial structure on the line was the three span bridge across the Trent at Lady Bay.

The route of the line at Eastcroft was lost within a couple of years of the tracks being lifted. The incinerator was completed in 1972.

Several design alternatives for the crossing were prepared, but the one finally settled upon was the design that maintained the tracks at the lowest possible level, whilst affording the maximum headroom for river traffic. The structure had three gracefully proportioned bowstring girders, with the deck suspended beneath. The flood arches on the approaches were in red brick with gritstone cappings, whilst the piers and cutwaters were clad with dressed limestone facings.

Other bridges on the line were to a variety of designs, but generally those over the railway tended to be masonry arches, whilst many of those beneath had steel decks. Four tunnels were needed on the route. The majority of these fell towards the south end of the line, as the route cut through the Leicestershire Wolds. One did fall in Nottinghamshire however. The tunnel at Stanton in the Wolds was a little over 1300yds long, and lined throughout its length.

The final remains of the Meadow Lane overbridge were removed in 1989 to make way for a warehouse development at the eastern side of the Cattle Market. In this view the undergrowth has been stripped ready for demolition of the arch.

An interesting consequence of the opening of the line was the appearance of Midland & Great Northern Railway trains at Nottingham for the first time. Locomotives turned out in their distinctive yellow ochre livery hauled trains from Midland Station to such exotic locations as Cromer and Yarmouth.

Passenger traffic generated by these wayside stations was not substantial, and Edwalton Station closed in 1941. The remainder closed their doors to passengers in 1949, although they remained open for freight services. There is evidence that British Railways even invested in modest expansion of goods facilities at Plumtree, with the construction of a prefabricated Provender store to supplement the single road goods shed. The investment was in vain however, with goods services being withdrawn in 1965. The line was earmarked for complete closure in the 1963 "Beeching" Report, presumably the view being taken that a direct rail service to London wasn't necessary. The London trains were diverted via Trent, and Nottingham effectively became a terminus again, at the end of a branch from the Erewash Valley line. All London trains had to reverse at Nottingham, and by 1966 the service to London was barely better than it had been a century before.

The junction at London Road was abolished in 1969, and the lines south finally lifted. It was not quite the end of the story for the line however. The tracks remained in situ to the south of Edwalton station and were used as a test track by British Rail. The line was upgraded and resignalled to accommodate high speed running, and 25Kv overhead electrification was provided. Over the following years it was to see many prototypes, including the gas-turbine APT, the later electric version and its eventual successor, the Pendolino. The most famous test on the line came in 1984 on the site of the goods yard at Old Dalby, when a nuclear flask wagon was crash tested. A withdrawn Class 46 diesel and rake of coaches were driven remotely at high speed into a flask wagon tipped on its side. The results were spectacular, and shown on national television news. The test was intended to show how safe it was to move nuclear products by rail, but critics slated it as a public relations stunt.

time low in this country, and Alstom, who leased the route for testing Pendolinos had no further use for the line. In late 2005 Network Rail announced that the facility would close, since they were not prepared to meet the costs of maintaining a dedicated 25kV test line. At the time of writing it is uncertain whether the route will be mothballed, or lifted. There may yet be, as there has before, an eleventh hour reprieve. The economic squeeze placed on Network Rail by the Government makes this seem unlikely.

Bridge No 3 is the most southerly structure to survive on the abandoned section of route. It carries the approach road to Lady Bay bridge, and the original parapets have been removed to accommodate a cantilevered footway, making the bridge wide enough to carry road traffic.

The Trent crossing was given a new lease of life in 1982 when it was converted to road use. The Lady Bay Bridge scheme connected what was then the A52, with Meadow Lane, significantly reducing the pressure on Trent Bridge. The chimney of Eastcroft Incinerator, built over the abandoned railway alignment is seen in the background.

Privatisation of the rail network may prove to be the final nail in the coffin of the line however. Since completion of the Pendolino test programme, the line has not been used. The development and manufacture of new trains has reached an all

There is hope that passenger services may yet return to the line. The South Notts Rail Study, drawn up by Nottinghamshire County Council includes an ambitious proposal to reconnect the line to Nottingham, via the disused colliery branch to Cotgrave. Trains would run via Rectory Junction at Colwick, to a new station at Cotgrave, and from there, along an entirely new section of railway, joining the old Midland route to the south of Tollerton.

The scheme would be linked to new park and ride sites, designed to take pressure off the crowded A52 and A606/A46 corridors. Unfortunately any such scheme requires a significant capital, and in the present climate this is not readily available. Given current procurement timescales, and even with Department for Transport approval the earliest that the scheme could become reality would be 2020.

On the abandoned section of route bridges were progressively removed over key roads, and the alignment was slowly reclaimed for housing. In 1972 a refuse incinerator was built across the disused alignment at Eastcroft, and in 1980 the disused bridge over the River Trent was refurbished, and converted into a road bridge. The last traces of Edwalton Station were demolished in the late Eighties, and a housing estate built on its site. As house and land prices have escalated, the pressure to redevelop has increased, and today in the southern suburbs there are few traces of the Midland's main line to London.

Plumtree Station building survives today as a restaurant. In the Eighties it stood derelict, but it was fortunately rescued and restored to a very high standard. The other railway buildings surviving here make this the most complete closed station on the line.

The A606 overbridge has been a problem to the Highway Authority for many years, owing to its restricted headroom. It was the site of a tragic accident in the early Nineties when an excavator on a low loader hit the bridge, and fell off. It struck an oncoming bus, causing fatalities amongst the passengers. Any projected scheme to join the Cotgrave Colliery branch to the Melton Line would connect to the south of here, rendering the bridge redundant and allowing its removal.

The level of attention to woodwork detail can clearly be seen in this view of the main station buildings. The stations never had BR enamelled signs. Waiting Rooms, Booking Offices and Refreshment Rooms all had individual cast iron letters screwed to their doors stating their different functions. In 1981 these were still in place, a century after being put there.

The goods shed at Plumtree is one of the most intact examples remaining in the County. It has been out of commercial use for a considerable period of time now, and sadly the years of neglect are starting to take their toll.

The spartan interior has changed little since railway days. The shed served as a shelter to load and unload perishable products from railway wagons into delivery drays. It had two large timber doors on the side, one for entry and one to exit by. The side doors ran on substantial cast iron wheels, whilst the end doors were suspended to clear the tracks.

In the early years after nationalisation, British Railways looked for ways to revitalise its dated goods handling facilities. One solution was the construction across the network of prefabricated asbestos-cement store buildings. "Provender" stores appeared around the country, usually at rural sites where no warehousing existed. Few have survived into modern times, making the example at Plumtree something of a rarity.

Bennett & Leese of Derby supplied the blue brick copings to the loading ramp edges at yards on the line. Their embossed markings are still clearly visible today.

The Down shelter has survived at Widmerpool, in a good state of repair and securely boarded, keeping out those who gain pleasure from destroying our heritage.

Widmerpool Station building has also survived, although it has been greatly modified, in a style that is not exactly sympathetic to the original structure. A single storey flat roofed extension occupies much of the Up platform, whilst the front edge of the down platform is gone.

Much of the Melton Line is equipped for state of the art high speed running. The permanent way is well maintained, the structures are in good order and the signalling is to current standards. Much of this former main line from Nottingham to London is arguably better equipped than the current route out to Trent. It is a shame that it seems destined to be abandoned at a time when pressure on train paths out of Nottingham is at an all time high.

7. The GCR south of the Trent

The character of the Great Central to the south of Nottingham was significantly different to that in the north. There were several reasons for this, but the key factors were geology and economics. To the north of the City, the route encountered sandstone and limestone, resulting in characteristic rock lined cuttings and tunnels through the northern outskirts and again at Kirkby in Ashfield.

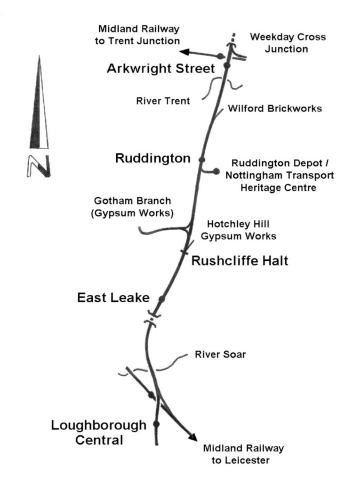

Above : Route map of the Great Central main line to the south of Nottingham. All connections and branches are shown, including the chord at Loughborough, opened in 1974 to facilitate closure north of Ruddington.

Extensive coal deposits resulted in a landscape dominated by collieries and plagued by subsidence. This was reflected in the lower speed limit of 75mph on the line in this area. The coalfields attracted other railway companies, so the route was crossed and joined by numerous lines and spurs.

The Great Central erected a substantial three span bridge to cross the Trent. Bridge 289 was a truss girder structure and carried goods lines in addition to the main lines. A signal box stood between the two sets of lines at the south end of the bridge. The structure provided a diving platform for the more adventurous local children for generations. This view was taken in 1984.

The route south traversed areas of Mercia Mudstone and glacial clays, requiring gently sloping earthworks. The exception to this was a ridge of Rhaetic Shale encountered near East Leake, through which a 99 yard tunnel was driven. The gently undulating landscape was, and still is predominantly agricultural in nature. Its stable geology also meant no subsidence and fewer speed limits than north of Victoria. Before the arrival of the Great Central there were, save a few gypsum tramways, no standard gauge railways due south of Nottingham.

Both parts of the Great Central fell within the Northern Division of the London Extension. The project was divided between three principal Civil Engineering Contractors, and one of the contract boundaries fell at East Leake. From here north to Annesley the works were constructed by Logan & Hemmingway, whilst south to Aylestone the works were built by Henry Lovatt.

Ground conditions at East Leake required careful timbering for the tunnel construction, and a brick invert was needed along the whole length of the structure.

Above : The total length of the Trent crossing was 830 feet, 400 of which comprised the three main river spans. The shallow depth of the deck was necessitated by headroom requirements stipulated by the Trent Navigation Company and the need to keep rail levels as low as possible. The length of the structure made photography difficult. This view is a composite of four shots.

Two photographs dating from around 1920, taken at Wilford by the late H E L Tatham.

Above : A Up express headed by a Class 8f (B4) leaves the smog of Nottingham in the distance at it heads south. Comprising of Barnum coaches, the train is probably bound for Marylebone.

Right : A lightweight Down express in the charge of a Class 9P (LNER Class B3) "Lord Faringdon" approaches the River Trent crossing.

Bridges on the route were in to a standardised design. Underbridges had masonry abutments and wing walls faced with Staffordshire brindled bricks. The decks comprised rivetted mild steel beams and troughing fabricated to a range of standard lengths, and parapets were open lattice steel. Where headroom permitted, the four main beams were placed beneath the rails. In cases where headroom was critical, three deeper beams were used, with the central one placed between the tracks and all projected above ground level. Overbridges were to one of two designs. The first of these was similar to the overbridge design with a steel deck, but brick jack arches in place of troughing. Solid parapets in brick or platework provided security for passing trains. The second design had arched masonry in lieu of the steel deck. This was used where deeper cuttings had to be crossed and frequently comprised three spans.

Rails were finally lifted at Wilford in 1974, and the route was abandoned. Wilford Road bridge was demolished almost immediately, owing to headroom problems. The remaining occupational bridges were left in place, including Bridge 292 near Bader Road. Movement of the abutments due to poor ground conditions has necessitated the insertion of props.

Nottingham City Council

Whilst the line was essentially rural in character, it was not altogether devoid of industry. At Wilford sidings were constructed to serve brickworks, and a two mile single track branch was built at Gotham to serve Gypsum workings. A connection to the plaster works at Hotchley Hill (Rushcliffe Halt) was built some years later, and when the Army constructed an Ordnance Depot at Ruddington, and this too was rail connected.

In keeping with company policy, few wayside stations were built between Nottingham and Loughborough. Initial provision was limited to just Ruddington and East Leake, but a halt would later be built at Hotchley Hill to provide workmen with access to the works there.

The first two of these stations were built to the standard island platform configuration, with a range of small buildings along the centreline, but no buildings at road level. Ruddington was accessed from an overbridge, whilst East Leake

was accessed through the abutment of an underbridge. Both stations were provided with goods yard facilities on the Up side of the running lines but neither had conventional goods sheds, being provided with small office buildings, and the space for a shed should the demand arise later. The halt at Hotchley Hill (Rushcliffe Halt) was built some years after the line opened, and was provided with two conventional platforms, rather than an island, in order to avoid disruption to the permanent way during construction.

The relatively short operational life of this superbly engineered line, and its tragic demise have been well documented elsewhere. What set this stretch of line apart however is what happened after the general closure of the London Extension.

The Ordnance Depot at Ruddington and the Plasterboard works at Hotchley Hill were both significant customers with no alternative means of moving heavy loads. A portion of the GC needed to be retained to facilitate these freight movements. The nearest junction with the remaining network was at Weekday Cross but it faced in the wrong direction and connected to another defunct line, The GNR route to Colwick, at Trent Lane Junction. This meant that trains from the old Midland Exchange Sidings at Nottingham faced two changes of direction before they could gain the Great Central.

By 1962, Wilford Brickworks sidings had gone, and the signal box controlling entry abolished. West Country Class Pacific No 30042 Sailsbury is seen here with a northbound special.

C A Hill

A single line was left in place, and this cumbersome arrangement was put into practice in 1968, continuing until May 1974 when British Rail built a chord from the erstwhile Midland main line at Loughborough to the disused alignment. The weed covered tracks were overhauled and freight services re-established. Gypsum and MOD trains were diverted to this reopened section, and the route from Ruddington to Nottingham was finally abandoned.

With the closure of Ruddington Depot in 1988, this just left dwindling gypsum traffic to support the line. It appeared that the end of the GCR in Nottinghamshire was in sight.

An unidentified 9F works a Down Relief past the site of Wilford Brickworks in 1964, watched by two young trainspotters from the far side of the cutting.

C A Hill

Occasionally in railway operation, a seemingly unrelated development can lead to unexpected benefits. Two sets of circumstances, each on the face of it negative, were to lead to a reprieve for the GCR.

A growing awareness of the affects of acid rain led to legislation forcing the CEGB to equip its coal burning power stations in the Trent Valley with flu gas desulphurisation equipment. This requires prodigious quantities of crushed limestone, to absorb the key pollutant, Sulphur Dioxide. The desulphurisation process converts the limestone into gypsum, and British Gypsum use this

industrial by-product in the manufacture of plasterboard. This arrangement has assured the future of the Hotchley Hill works, and significant maintenance works have been carried out to the remaining track to ensure that it can handle the increase in traffic.

The second development arose from the demise of Ruddington Depot. The County Council's plans to create a country park at the site offered a one-off opportunity to try and preserve the section of the GCR to the north of Loughborough. A break-away group from the preserved railway at Loughborough formulated a proposal to create a new railway centre at the Ruddington site. This would utilise the junction with the main line, and some of the existing MoD buildings. Trains would run initially to Rushcliffe Halt, with a longer term aim to reopen the whole length to passenger trains. Fortunately the County and District Councils were sympathetic to their cause, and the seeds of the Nottingham Transport Heritage Centre were sown.

By 1990 the alignment was becoming quite overgrown. This view of Ruddington Lane overbridge (No 295) contrasts with the previous picture, where it is visible in the background. The bridge was infilled and the steel parapets demolished in the mid Nineties.

The Centre has become home to a fine collection of old Nottingham buses, and the site of an extensive miniature railway, but it is the standard gauge railway that arguably draws most interest. The connection into the site has been overhauled, and a platform built to allow short passenger trains to run, hauled by a variety of shunting locomotives. A number of larger main line locomotives have also visited the centre, drawing considerable attention. Facilities continue to develop and a fine two road engine shed has been built, and Neasden South signal box re-erected at the site. The Centre is gradually gaining ground as a tourist attraction and seems destined for long term success.

The immediate aim of running trains to the old station at Hotchley Hill (Rushcliffe Halt) has been achieved, and weekend access to the line south to the River Soar crossing near Loughborough has also been successfully negotiated, avoiding conflict with gypsum workings. Despite East Leake station platform remaining intact, it seems unlikely that it can be fully reopened. Sole access to it is from a blind bend on a busy road with a poor standard of footway, and the goods yard was redeveloped for housing in the 1980s, eliminating the only other potential access point. It is also unlikely that Ruddington Station will be incorporated into the preservation venture for similar reasons.

In the final years of the London Extension, passenger workings were often handled by diesel units. A southbound train passes the site of Wilford Brickworks in 1964. Tracks here would be finally lifted ten years later.

C A Hill

The long term aspirations are to replace the missing bridge across the Midland Railway at Loughborough, and link up with the established section of preserved Great Central running south from Loughborough. Once connected, the two sections will form the longest preserved line in the country, connecting the

outskirts of Leicester with the outskirts of Nottingham. As the only preserved main line, and with a connection to Network Rail, the potential of this ambitious scheme is clear.

Wilwell Cutting, between Wilford and Ruddington has become home to many species of flora and fauna. It has been classified as a Site of Special Scientific Interest and is now a nature reserve. The cutting is immediately south of the section of route safeguarded for a light rail scheme, and may yet see use again. The bridge seen here is No 296.

The railway heritage movement is not the only body to look at use of the old Great Central for rail transport. The alignment from the Trent, south to Silverdale has been safeguarded for potential light rail use by the Local Authority since the late 1980s. The realisation of the first phase of Nottingham's NET (Nottingham Express Transit) system has brought a new lease of life to the route a step closer. Plans are presently to join the old GCR route at Coronation Avenue, and construct a tramway to the east of the GC embankment at Wilford, before slewing onto the old railway alignment at Wilford Lane. From here, the trams would follow the line of the railway, beneath Ruddington Lane and the A52, before deviating to cross fields near Silverdale, and on into Clifton.

The success of NET Line One and the growing congestion on the roads make an extension of NET likely, although the timescale of procuring this could prove to be long drawn. It is entirely possible that some sections of the abandoned GCR will carry rails again, as part of a Twenty first Century state of the art transport system.

At Ruddington more tangible remains can still be found. In the spring of 1980 the Down main line and goods road were still in place, and in reasonable order. The station buildings had gone, but much of the platform remained together with some interesting signalling relics.

To the south of Ruddington, the Ordnance Depot line branched east. By 1988 trains into the site had finished, and the rails were becoming overgrown. The main line is seen to the right, beneath the footbridge (No 299).

H E L Tatham

Rushcliffe Halt was still relatively new when this photograph was taken, shortly before the Grouping. An Up express in the charge of a Class 9P (B3) is seen approaching the station.

H E L Tatham

At Hotchley Hill, sidings were built to serve the Marblelite works. A halt was also constructed, primarily for workers, although it did appear in the public timetable. A "Jersey Lily" Atlantic is seen pulling away from Rushcliffe Halt in about 1920, with a Down express.

H E L Tatham

By 1988 passenger trains were long gone. Rushcliffe halt retained its platforms, although the original timber construction seen above had been replaced by concrete. Bridge No 308 remained in good order, but the steel footbridge between the platforms had been removed.

After Rushcliffe Halt closed, the platform shelters were demolished, and the footbridge removed. The Down line remained in use for freight, whilst a substantial length of the Up line remained as a loop, preserving the "main line" feel of the location. The signal box was built during LNER operation, and is probably contemporary with the concrete platforms.

East Leake Station was cleared of platform buildings after closure, but the platform itself remained in remarkably good condition.

Goods provision was minimal at many of the wayside stations, since pick-up goods trains were not seen as a priority. In 1988 the original office and timber shed remained in place. A few years later they were demolished to make way for housing.

The Down line was lifted here in about 1969, but the signals were not recovered, despite being relatively new. The Goods Office can be seen beyond the platform.

Access to East Leake was via a staircase in the south (left) abutment of Bridge 312 crossing the main road from East to West Leake. Poor accessibility may prove the deciding factor in whether this station is ever reopened.

Appendix 1

Speed Limits on the GCR in Nottinghamshire.

Extracts from LNER Working Regs, May 1942.

Leicester and Nottingham	Up and Down lines	75
Ruddington	Over Factory Branch	20
*Weekday Cross Junction and Nottingham Vic. Station.	Down line	10
Nottingham Vic. Station	All lines through station	10
*Carrington and Nottingham Vic. Station.	Up line	10
Bagthorpe Junction (77¾ miles) and Carrington.	Up line	60
Bagthorpe Junction and Basford East Junction.	... ...	15
Bulwell South Junction	To and from Branches	10
Bulwell North Junction	Up line	20
and Bestwood Junction ...	Down line	10
Annesley North Junction	To and from Leen Valley line	10
Kirkby South Junction	To and from Mansfield line	30
,, ,, ,, ...	To and from Leen Valley line	10
Tibshelf	Curve at 64 miles—Up line	65
	Down line	60

Appendix 2

Special Instructions for working the Gotham Branch.

Extracts from LNER Working Regulations.

RUDDINGTON.

GOTHAM BRANCH.

The single line from Gotham sidings to Shepherd's No. 2 siding is worked in accordance with the Regulations for Working Single Lines by One Engine in Steam, etc., and the train staff is kept at Gotham Sidings Signal Box. The level crossing gates at East Leake Road and Kegworth Road stand normally across the Railway. Drivers must bring their train to a stand near the gates at each of the level crossings and the Shunter must open the gates for the train to pass over, and close and lock them after the last vehicle is clear. During shunting operations at Gotham Company's siding the Shunter is responsible for passing road traffic over East Leake Road crossing. The points leading into Gotham Company's siding, Shepherd's Nos. 1 and 2 sidings from the single line, are padlocked, and the keys of the points, also of the crossing gates, are kept at Ruddington Station.

Appendix 3

Special Instructions for working the Nottingham to Grantham line.

Extracts from LNER Working Regulations.

ASLOCKTON.

ENGINES TAKING WATER.

Drivers of Up Freight trains requiring to take water at Aslockton must give **one crow** whistle on passing Saxondale Junction Box, or in the case of such trains stopping on the Goods line, as soon as it is known that water will be required at Aslockton. The Signalman at the Junction Box to advise Aslockton accordingly.

Drivers of Up trains desiring to obtain water at Aslockton must bring their trains to a stand on the west side, and clear of station level crossing. The engine must then be detached and go forward to the water crane. (D.6834).

Drivers of all Down Freight trains, the engines of which require to take water at Aslockton, must whistle **one crow** when passing Allington Junction, and the Signalman at that place must advise Bottesford West and Elton that the train concerned requires to stop at Aslockton for water.

Drivers of Down trains desiring to obtain water at Aslockton must bring their trains to a stand on the east side and clear of the station level crossing. The engine must be detached and go forward to the water crane. Guards must be careful to secure the trains before the engines are detached.

TRAINS STOPPED AT UP STARTING SIGNAL.

When the Aslockton Up Starting signal is at danger, Drivers must, when the weather is sufficiently clear to enable them to do so, bring their engines to a stand about 30 yards before reaching the Station Master's house, and must wait there until the signal is lowered, unless instructed to the contrary by the Signalman.

SAXONDALE.

When one or more light engines are coupled to a Freight train, and it is necessary to turn the train on the Slow road, and that road is blocked, the light engine or engines must be uncoupled before entering the Slow road, and sent Main line at first opportunity.

RADCLIFFE-ON-TRENT.

TRAINMEN'S CABIN.

A cabin is provided near the Down Home signal at Radcliffe-on-Trent for the use of train reliefmen. A telephone is installed therein which gives communication with Radcliffe-on-Trent Box and the Control Office. When it is desired to speak to the Control, place the switch to position "Control," and speak. To communicate with the Radcliffe-on-Trent Box, place switch to position "Signal box," turn handle and speak.

No. 28 OCCUPATION LEVEL CROSSING.

To avoid, as far as possible, the blocking of the above crossing (which is situate 340 yards east of the Down Goods line Home signal) when a train is standing at that signal, a following train must stop clear of the crossing, and about 20 yards from the brake of the first train if the latter is standing on the crossing. (D.6071).

Appendix 4

Signal Box Opening hours
Extracts from LMR Nottingham Area, December 1969.

SIGNAL BOX	HOURS OPEN
TRENT TO NEWARK CASTLE STATION (ER)	
Sneinton Crossing	10 30 Sunday to T.O.S. last train Sat/Sun (Summer) 13 45 Sunday to T.O.S. last train Sat/Sun (Winter)
Trent Lane Crossing	Continuously
Colwick Crossing	10 30 Sunday to T.O.S. last train Sat/Sun (Summer) 13 45 Sunday to T.O.S. last train Sat/Sun (Winter)
Netherfield Junction	10 30 Sunday to T.O.S. last train Sat/Sun (Summer) 14 00 Sunday to T.O.S. last train Sat/Sun (Winter)
** Carlton & Netherfield	03 10 Monday to T.O.S. for last train Saturday *0015 Sunday* 14 00 to T.O.S. for last train Sunday *2320 Sunday*
Burton Joyce L.C.	Continuously
** Lowdham	03 10 Monday to T.O.S. for last train Saturday *000f Sunday* 14 00 to T.O.S. last train Sunday *2370 Sunday*
Thurgarton L.C.	Continuously
Fiskerton	06 00 to 21 50 Monday to Friday 06 00 to T.O.S. for last train Saturday. 14 00 to 21 50 Sunday
** Staythorpe Crossing	03 15 Monday to T.O.S. for last train Sat/Sun. 14 00 to T.O.S. last train Sunday
Newark Castle Station	Eastern Region
LENTON SOUTH JUNCTION TO LENTON NORTH JUNCTION	
Lenton South Junction (Controlled by Trent Power Box)	See page 37
Lenton North Junction (Controlled by Trent Power Box)	See below
NOTTINGHAM, MANSFIELD JUNCTION TO TROWELL JUNCTION	
Mansfield Junction (Controlled by Trent PB)	See page 35
Lenton North Junction (Controlled by Trent PB)	See page 35
Radford Junction (Controlled by Trent PB)	See page 35
Trowell Junction (Controlled by Trent PB)	See page 35

RADFORD JUNCTION TO SHIREBROOK WEST) SIDINGS	
Radford Junction	See page 38
** Lincoln Street Crossing	06 00 Monday to 13 50 Saturday
Basford Junction	06 00 Monday to 13 50 Saturday
** Bulwell Forest Crossing	06 00 Monday to 13 50 Saturday
Bestwood Park Junction	06 00 Monday to 13 50 Saturday
Hucknall Colliery Sidings	06 00 Monday to 13 50 Saturday
** Linby Colliery Sidings	06 00 Monday to 13 50 Saturday
** Linby Station	06 00 Monday to 13 50 Saturday
Annesley	06 00 Monday to 13 50 Saturday
** Kirkby-in-Ashfield Station Junction	05 30 Monday to 13 50 Saturday
** Kirkby-in-Ashfield Sidings	05 30 Monday to 13 50 Saturday
** Sutton Junction	05 45 Monday to 13 50 Saturday
** Mansfield South Junction *{ 0600-2200 M/F { 0600-1400 SAT }*	05 45 Monday to 13 50 Saturday
Sherwood Colliery Sidings South	06 00 Monday to 13 50 Saturday
Shirebrook West Sidings	Eastern Region
MANSFIELD SOUTH JN. TO RUFFORD COLLIERY (ER)	
** Mansfield South Junction	See above
** Mansfield Colliery Junction	06 00 to 21 50 Monday to Friday 06 00 to 13 50 Saturday
** Rufford Colliery Sidings	Eastern Region
EAST LEAKE TO NOTTINGHAM, WEEKDAY CROSS JUNCTION	
East Leake	07 45 to 15 35 Monday to Friday
Hotchley Hill	Open as required (07 45 to 15 35 Monday to Friday)
Gotham Sidings	Open as required (07 45 to 15 35 Monday to Friday)
Ruddington	07 45 to 15 35 Monday to Friday
** Weekday Cross Junction	See page 40
ASLOCKTON (ER) TO NETHERFIELD JUNCTION	
Aslockton Station	Eastern Region
** Bingham	05 15 Monday to TOS for last train/i.e. Saturday/Sunday
(Summer)	10 30 to TOS for last train Sunday
(Winter)	14 00 to TOS for last train Sunday

Bibliography

Whilst numerous information sources were used during the research of this book, specific reference was made to the following publications and documents. Every effort has been made to ensure that information is reproduced correctly, however any errors or omissions are wholly the Author's responsibility.

Institution of Civil Engineers
Paper No 3227 20th March 1900
The Great Central Railway : Northern Division
F W Bidder

Great Northern Railway Act 1880
Indicative Alignment Plans
(Reproduced from Ordnance Survey Mapping)

The Great Northern Railway
O S Nock

The Midland Railway
C Hamilton-Ellis

History of the Midland Counties Railway
C T Goode

The Great Northern Railway in the East Midlands Vols 1-4
A Henshaw

The Midland Railway around Nottinghamshire Vol 1
G Hurst

Passengers No More
G Daniels & L Dench

An Illustrated History of Great Northern Railway Signalling
M A Vanns

The Development of Nottingham's Railways
J P Wilson

The Railways of Newark on Trent
M A Vanns

Signalling Atlas & Signal Box Directory of Great Britain & Ireland
P Kay

The Great Central Then & Now
M Hawkins

Ordnance Survey 1954 Edition 1:2500 mapping.

Acknowledgements

The Author is indebted to the following individuals, organisations and companies for their assistance during the writing of this book. Their contributions, through allowing access to private collections and unpublished reference material, and arranging permission to visit restricted sites has considerably elevated the status of the completed work and broadened the Author's knowledge along the way.

Ian Askew
Geoff Brain
John Bull
Tom Hawkins
Ian Trivett
John Mulhall
Building Design Partnership
BWB Consulting Ltd
Eastside & City
Greenhatch Building Surveys Ltd
Laing O'Rourke
Network Rail
Nottingham (Bulwell) MRS
Nottingham City Council